Warrior · 72

Imperial Roman Legionary AD 161–284

Ross Cowan · Illustrated by Angus McBride

First published in Great Britain in 2003 by Osprey Publishing,
Elms Court, Chapel Way, Botley, Oxford OX2 9LP, UK.
Email: info@ospreypublishing.com

A CIP catalogue record for this book is available from the British Library

ISBN 1 84176 601 1

Ross Cowan has asserted his/her right under the Copyright, Designs and
Patents Act, 1988, to be identified as the Author of this Work

Editor: Gerard Barker
Design: Ken Vail Graphic Design, Cambridge, UK
Index by Alan Thatcher
Originated by Grasmere Digital Imaging, Leeds, UK
Printed in China through World Print Ltd.

03 04 05 06 07   10 9 8 7 6 5 4 3 2 1

FOR A CATALOGUE OF ALL BOOKS PUBLISHED BY OSPREY MILITARY AND
AVIATION PLEASE CONTACT:

The Marketing Manager, Osprey Direct UK, PO Box 140,
Wellingborough, Northants, NN8 2FA, United Kingdom.
Email: info@ospreydirect.co.uk

The Marketing Manager, Osprey Direct USA,
c/o MBI Publishing, PO Box 1, 729 Prospect Ave,
Osceola, WI 54020, USA.
Email: info@ospreydirectusa.com

Buy online at www.ospreypublishing.com

Artist's note

Readers may care to note that the original paintings from
which the colour plates in this book were prepared are
available for private sale. All reproduction copyright
whatsoever is retained by the Publishers. All enquiries
should be addressed to:

Angus McBride
26 Hastings Place
Durban Road
Wynberg (Chelsea Village)
Cape Town
South Africa

The Publishers regret that they can enter into no
correspondence upon this matter.

Author's note

The author would like to thank the Cowan family, Ged
Barker, Donal Bateson, Rebecca Cullen, Megan Doyan, Tom
Lowres, Thomas McGrory, Marjeta Šašel-Kos, Krista Ubbels
and Susan Walker. Thanks also to the Hunterian Museum at
the University of Glasgow, Yale University Art Gallery, the
British Museum and the Regional Museum in Celje,
Slovenia, for photographic material.

Special thanks to Duncan Campbell and Simon James for
valuable advice concerning the siege of Dura-Europos;
Steven D.P. Richardson for his sketches and help with
preparation of the photographic material for this and the
previous *Roman Legionary* volume and Kathleen
McLaughlin for her translations of Zonaras and Dexippus.
Lawrence Keppie read a draft of the text and offered
valuable suggestions. Any errors remain the author's.

Please note that translated quotations are adapted from the
Loeb Classical Library unless otherwise stated.

CONTENTS

IMPERIAL ROMAN LEGIONARY AD 161–284

INTRODUCTION

Between AD 161 and 284 the Roman legions were involved in wars and battles on an epic scale. Legions were destroyed in battle (e.g. IX Hispana), disbanded for rebellion (III Augusta), and formed to wage wars of conquest and defence (II, III Italica, I–III Parthica). For the first time a legion was stationed in Italy itself. Legio II Parthica, raised by Septimius Severus in 193–94, was based at Albanum near Rome and as the emperor's personal legion became one of the most important units in the empire. Above all, this was a period of crisis. The Empire faced unprecedented assaults by Germans, Goths and Persians, and suffered doubly from ceaseless civil wars. The legionary system almost broke under the strain, yet by the close of this period, the Romans had defeated their major enemies and reunited the empire. This was achieved with armies based on legionary vexillations (combat detachments), led by emperors who had risen from the ranks of the army, and were determined not to repeat the mistakes of the past.

This book enlarges on the themes raised in *Roman Legionary, 58 BC–AD 69* (Warrior 71). Using legio II Parthica as a central focus, it considers the development of elite troops, such as *lanciarii*; the growing use of vexillations instead of whole legions going to war; developments in equipment; the archaeology of battle using Dura-Europos as a case

Distance slab recording the construction of 3,000ft of the Antonine Wall by a vexillation of legio XX Valeria Victrix ('Valiant and Victorious'), c.142. The central panel shows a goddess, perhaps Victory, placing a wreath in the beak of the legion's eagle standard. (Hunterian Museum, University of Glasgow)

study, and the implications of the legalisation of soldiers' marriages and issues such as military-owned prostitutes. To avoid repetition of evidence used in *Roman Legionary, 58 BC–AD 69*, relevant sections in that work are referred to by *RL* followed by page number(s).

CHRONOLOGY

AD 161 Marcus Aurelius and Lucius Verus become emperors. A legion (perhaps IX Hispana) is destroyed by Parthians in Armenia.

162–66 Romans victorious in Parthian War; new territory annexed in Middle East but soldiers returning from the East bring plague to Europe which recurs throughout the late 2nd and 3rd centuries.

163–67 Evacuation of the Antonine Wall in central Scotland.

165 Formation of legions II and III Italica.

167–80 Marcomannic and Sarmatian wars. Death of Verus (169). Ultimately successful Roman campaigns; Commodus abandons plans to annex new territory beyond the Danube when Marcus Aurelius dies in 180.

180–84 Intermittent fighting across the Danube and in Dacia.

185–86 Revolt of Maternus and deserters in Gaul.

192 Commodus murdered; Pertinax recognised as emperor by Senate (31 December).

193 Pertinax murdered by Praetorian Guard; Didius Julianus bribes praetorians and becomes emperor. Pescennius Niger, governor of Syria, and Septimius Severus, governor of Pannonia, proclaimed emperors by their respective provincial armies; Severus recognises Clodius Albinus, governor of Britain, as his Caesar (April). Severus marches on Rome, Julianus murdered and praetorians disbanded; new Praetorian Guard created from men transferred from the legions (June).

193–94 Severus' generals victorious over Niger at Perinthus, Cyzicus, Nicaea and Issus. Niger captured and executed attempting to escape to Parthia.

194–95 Severus campaigns against Parthian vassal states that aided Niger. Creation of province of Osrhoene; legions I, II and III Parthica established.

196–97 Clodius Albinus invades Gaul and German provinces, finally defeated at Lugdunum (Lyon) in February 197.

197–99 Severus invades Parthia; Ctesiphon captured and burned. New province of Mesopotamia established. Two attempts to capture Hatra fail.

203–4 Severus campaigns in North Africa, advancing frontier to the Sahara.

208–11 Severus invades northern Britain determined to complete the conquest of the island. Severus dies at York (211). His sons Caracalla and Geta assume full power.

212 Caracalla murders Geta (February); *Constitutio Antoniniana* grants Roman citizenship to all freeborn inhabitants of the empire.

212–15 Severan outposts in Scotland evacuated.

213 Caracalla defeats Cenni and Alamanni.

214 Caracalla campaigns against Free Dacians.

215 Preparations for Parthian War; massacre at Alexandria.

216 Caracalla invades Adiabene and sacks Arbela, desecrating the tombs of the Parthian kings.

217 Caracalla murdered on road between Carrhae and Edessa. Praetorian prefect Opellius Macrinus proclaimed emperor. Romans and Parthians fight indecisive battle at Nisibis.

218 Macrinus defeated by Elagabalus outside Antioch and killed whilst attempting to flee to Europe.

222 Praetorians murder the insane Elagabalus. Severus Alexander succeeds as emperor.

224–26 Ardashir of Persia defeats his Parthian overlords; new Sassanian Persian era.

228–29 Ardashir fails to take Hatra, now reinforced by Romans. He invades Roman Mesopotamia. Some Roman troops kill the provincial prefect and desert to Ardashir.

231–33 Severus Alexander campaigns against Ardashir. Mesopotamia recaptured and Romans successful in Armenia and Media but Ardashir defeats a third Roman army near Ctesiphon.

233–34 Alamanni and other Germannic confederations raid Roman provinces.

235 Severus Alexander attempts to negotiate with Alamanni and is murdered by disgusted troops. Maximinus proclaimed emperor and defeats the Alamanni. Maximinus is the first Roman emperor to fight in battle.

236–37 Maximinus defeats Sarmatians and Carpi.

238 Rebellion over tax collection in Africa. Gordian, proconsul of Africa proclaimed emperor with his son, but they are defeated in battle by legio III Augusta outside Carthage. Senate in Rome elects from its ranks Balbinus and Pupienus as emperors. Maximinus invades Italy and unexpectedly fails to storm Aquileia. His troops become mutinous and he is murdered. Praetorians in Rome grow weary of Balbinus and Pupienus, whom they murder and elevate Gordian III (grandson of the proconsul) as a puppet emperor.

238–41 Persians seize Roman Mesopotamia and Hatra; Shapur I succeeds Ardashir (241). Barbarian invasions across Danube.

242–44 Romans under praetorian prefect Timesitheus defeat Persians at Rhesaina and recover Mesopotamia (243). Timesitheus dies of natural causes and Philip becomes prefect. Roman invasion of Persia meets with disaster outside Ctesiphon; Gordian III is mortally wounded but Philip is suspected of having him killed. Philip proclaimed emperor. He buys peace from Shapur.

245	Philip defeats the Carpi; warfare on the Danube (245–47).
247	Philip celebrates Rome's 1,000th anniversary with great games and spectacles.
248–49	Philip sends Decius to Pannonia to quell rebellions. The Pannonian legions proclaim Decius emperor. Philip killed in battle against Decius at Verona (249).
250–51	Decius defeated by Goths under Kniva (250). Again pursuing the Gothic raiders he is killed with his son and much of his field army at Abrittus (251). Trebonianus Gallus succeeds. He purchases peace from the Goths but is unable to pay tribute to Shapur who invades Roman territory.
252–53	Shapur destroys a Roman field army mustering at Barbalissos and captures Antioch.
253	Aemilianus defeats Carpi and is proclaimed emperor by his troops. Gallus sends Valerian to gather an army to oppose him. Gallus is murdered by his own troops when they find themselves outnumbered by Aemilianus; he is subsequently murdered by his soldiers at the approach of Valerian's army. Valerian is proclaimed emperor. He makes his son Gallienus co-emperor.
253–60	Gallienus and his sons campaign with success against Germans and Goths on Rhine and Danube frontiers. Valerian restores his eastern provinces but Shapur invades in 253 and 260 capturing Antioch on both occasions. Valerian's army is defeated by Shapur outside Edessa in 260. The emperor and tens of thousands of Roman troops are taken into Persian captivity. Remnants of the Roman forces are rallied by Macrianus and Ballista who harry Shapur's forces. The younger Macriani are proclaimed emperors

but are defeated by Gallienus' forces in Thrace and by Odaenathus of Palmyra in Syria (261). Palmyra subsequently dominates the eastern provinces and forms breakaway empire of Syria, Arabia and Egypt (267–72).

258–60	Gallienus defeats the Alamanni; his son, Saloninus is killed at Cologne and Postumus forms breakaway Gallic Empire based on Gaul, the Germanies, Britain and Spain (in existence 259–74).
268	Gallienus defeats the Goths but is the victim of a plot headed by senior officers including Claudius and Aurelian. Claudius becomes emperor.
269	Claudius destroys Gothic invaders at Naissus; dies of plague (270).
270–75	Aurelian becomes emperor. He defeats the Iuthungi, Iazyges and Goths (270–71), and proceeds to defeat the Palmyrene and Gallic empires and the Carpi (272–74). He is murdered as a result of a court plot whilst preparing to attack Persia.
276–82	Probus eventually becomes emperor. He repels the Alamanni and Franks from Gaul, and Burgundians and Vandals from Raetia (277–80). He campaigns against bandits and nomads in Asia and Egypt (280–81). He is murdered at the instigation of his praetorian prefect, Carus.
282–84	Carus invades Persia and captures Ctesiphon but is apparently struck by lightning when he attempts to advance beyond the city. His son Carinus dies in suspicious circumstances as the army retreats to Roman territory. Diocles, commander of the bodyguards, is proclaimed emperor.
285	Diocles defeats Numerianus, son of Carus, at Margus. He takes the name Diocletian and the Roman recovery begins.

THE FORMATION OF NEW LEGIONS, AD 161–284

When Marcus Aurelius and his co-emperor Lucius Verus assumed power in 161 there were 29 legions in the Roman army, but almost immediately news came that a legion, perhaps the famous IX Hispana, had been destroyed in battle against the Parthians (Dio, 71.2.1). The legion was not replaced for the subsequent war against the Parthians (162–66); it was not until 165 that Marcus Aurelius enrolled new legions, II and III Italica ('Italian'), to face the coming German menace on the northern frontiers (Dio, 55.24.5).

The new legions of our period were raised by conscription, though a number of volunteers were attracted by the prospect of good pay and promotion. This process was known as the *dilectus* or levy. *Dilectus* are recorded in northern Italy in connection with the formation of legions II and III Italica. The number of legions remained at 30 until Septimius Severus raised the three Parthian legions in *c.*194. Legions I and III Parthica were probably formed out of the mass of Syrian conscripts levied by Pescennius Niger and were without unit or purpose following his defeat in 194 (Kennedy, 1987). The most famous legion, II Parthica, was partly raised by conscription in Italy as early as 193 (note Herodian,

2.14.5–7). Inscriptions referring to levies in northern Italy held under Alexander Severus and Maximinus (*c*.231–38) might refer to the recruitment of legio IV Italica, but it is disputed whether the legion was formed before the close of the 3rd century (Brunt, 1974). It may have been traditional to raise new legions in Italy, but it supplied very few recruits to established legions after the first century AD (Mann, 1963 & 1999). Legio II Parthica was exceptional in having considerable numbers of Italians in its ranks, but this was because it was based in Italy. Long-established legions based in the provinces drew heavily on the local populations and sometimes beyond the frontier.

Herodian's description of Caracalla's visit to Alexandria in AD 215 illustrates how a *dilectus* might be conducted:

> [Caracalla] issued an edict that all the young men should assemble on an open area of ground, saying that he wished to enrol a phalanx in honour of Alexander [the Great] … The young men were told to muster in ranks so that the emperor could examine each man and decide how far his age, size and condition were up to the army's standard. (Herodian, 4.9.4–5, after Whittaker, 1969–70)

Herodian tells us that Caracalla's Alexandrian levy was simply a ploy to gather the young men of the city in one place so that they might be massacred. The Alexandrians had apparently made Caracalla the butt of many jokes and that he desired revenge. What actually happened in Alexandria is uncertain but an inscription set up by a centurion of legio II Parthica gives thanks for his survival of 'the Alexandrian dangers'

ABOVE LEFT **Gravestone of Vitalis, a German transferred from legio I Minervia into the Praetorian Guard. He died *c*.217. He is armed with a weighted *pilum* with a bound shaft, and an eagle-hilted sword, perhaps a gift from the emperor. Museo Archeologico, Fiesole. (Steven D.P. Richardson)**

ABOVE RIGHT **Gravestone of Aurelius Iustinus, soldier of legio II Italica, killed during a campaign against the Dacians, 3rd century AD. His weighted *pilum* and oval shield (note the central reinforcing bar) are slung over his back. (By courtesy of the Regional Museum, Celje, Slovenia)**

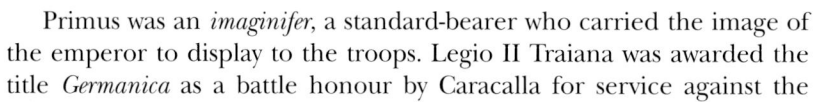

ABOVE **Panel on the much eroded Arch of Severus in Rome (c.203) showing a ram being used to assault the walls of Ctesiphon whilst a *testudo* advances against the city in 197. Above the emperor Septimius Severus addresses his troops. (Author's collection)**

RIGHT **Legionary *antoninianus* of Gallienus (c.259/60), depicting legio III Italica's stork emblem. (Hunter Coin Cabinet, University of Glasgow)**

(Bruun 1995). There was certainly serious street fighting in the city which might have been caused when unwilling conscripts rioted but the abuse directed at Caracalla may disguise an actual rebellion in the city during the absence of its legion, II Traiana, in 213:

> Quintus Iulius Primus, *imaginifer* soldier of legio II Traiana Germanica fortis [brave] Antoniniana, served 22 years, born in Africa at Theveste, transferred from legio III Augusta pia vindex [loyal and avenging], lived 45 years. Aurelia Dioscurus had this made for her beloved husband. (*ILS* 2319)

Primus was an *imaginifer*, a standard-bearer who carried the image of the emperor to display to the troops. Legio II Traiana was awarded the title *Germanica* as a battle honour by Caracalla for service against the

Cenni, a Germanic people (213). II Traiana was the only legion so honoured during the war and must have performed exceptionally in battle. The legion's other title, *Antoniniana*, was derived from the official name of Caracalla, Antoninus, and essentially means 'Antoninus' own'. Primus was transferred from the Numidian legion III Augusta, whose titles *pia vindex* ('loyal, avenging') were granted by Septimius Severus when the legion supported his bid for power in 193. Primus' transfer may have occurred before the war in order to bring the unit up to fighting strength; during, if III Augusta also supplied troops to the field army; or after, to make good casualties sustained in the war. It is probable that all new legions were built around such cadres of trained legionaries transferred from other units. Veteran centurions were certainly detailed with the command and training of these new formations.

The army usually preferred recruits from agricultural backgrounds rather than city-dwellers like the Alexandrians, because such men were familiar with hard work and tough conditions (cf. Vegetius, *Epitome*, 1.3). It was the provincial and predominantly rural background of legionaries that led the gravestone of a praetorian centurion to sneer that he had 'faithfully commanded a century in a praetorian cohort, not in a barbarian legion' (*ILS* 2671; Keppie 1997: 99). The legionaries had the last laugh. In 193 Septimius Severus dishonourably discharged the entire Praetorian Guard for its part in the murder of the emperor Pertinax, and re-formed it from soldiers drawn from the legions (Dio, 74.2.3–6; Herodian, 2.14.5).

The appearance and manners of such rural soldiers shocked the senator Dio. Familiar with the relatively cultured praetorians, he reports that the Pannonian legionaries who entered Rome with Septimius Severus in 193 were 'most savage in appearance, most terrifying in speech, and most boorish in conversation', but he admitted that they were by far the better soldiers (Dio, 74.2.3–6).

Evidence from gravestones suggests that most legionaries enlisted between the ages of 17 and 23, but older and younger recruits were not

ABOVE LEFT **Legionary *antoninianus* of Gallienus (c.259/60), showing legio II Parthica's centaur emblem. (Hunter Coin Cabinet, University of Glasgow)**

ABOVE RIGHT ***Denarius* of Septimius Severus commemorating legio XIV Gemina's role in Severus' successful march on Rome, AD 193. The legion's eagle standard is flanked by two centurial standards. (Hunter Coin Cabinet, University of Glasgow)**

uncommon. Vegetius states that the ideal height of a legionary was 6 Roman feet (5ft 9in; 1.77m). He adds that the legionaries of the first cohort should be at least 5 Roman feet and 10 inches (5ft 7in; 1.72m) (Vegetius, *Epitome*, 1.5). His figures are complemented by the skeletons of two soldiers found in a double grave at Canterbury dating to *c*.200. One man was aged about 30 and 1.73m tall (5ft 8 in), the other was aged about 20 and 1.815m tall (5ft 11 in). His skeleton was better preserved and indicated that he had been particularly muscular. The soldiers appear to have been murdered (Bennett et al. 1982: 46, 191).

TERMS OF SERVICE

Length of service

In the mid-1st century AD service in the legions was fixed at 25 years, but the practice of discharging soldiers every second year rather than annually meant that about half of them served for 26 years before *honesta missio* (honourable discharge) was granted. Biennial discharges were still in effect during the reign of Marcus Aurelius (161–80), but early in the reign of Septimius Severus (193–211) discharge became an annual occurrence and all legionaries served for 26 years.

Soldiers of legio II Parthica were still discharged after 26 years' service in 244 (*AE* 1981: 134), but this date marks the accession of the emperor Philip and a 40-year period of continual foreign and civil wars and soldiers were kept in service long beyond the usual term. Consequently, during the reign of Aurelian (270–75) we find a soldier named Aurelius Iulianus who had served in legio II Parthica for 33 years (*AE* 1975: 171). He was probably conscripted during the reign of Gordian III for the Persian war of 242–44.

Pay

'A soldier is not to be feared if he is clothed, armed, shod, has a full belly, and some money in his purse.' (Historia Augusta, *Severus Alexander*, 52.3)

Septimius Severus was the first emperor to increase military pay since Domitian (81–96). Domitian's basic annual rate was 300 silver *denarii* paid in four instalments. Under-officers (*principales*) such as *tesserarii* (officers of the watchword) received pay and a half, but the more senior *optio* and *signifer* were *duplicarii* and received double pay or rations. Severus increased pay for all soldiers in 197 in celebration of his victory over Clodius Albinus at Lugdunum. The rate of increase is unknown but is presumed to be 50 per cent, thus increasing basic pay to 450 *denarii*. This was a large sum but it is difficult to equate to modern values. However, unlike the majority of the Empire's inhabitants who lived at subsistence level, the soldier usually had enough money to maintain his family and buy luxury goods or even slaves. His pay was also supplemented by 'donatives', special gifts of gold or silver coin or bullion, rations and clothing made on the emperor's accession day or given in place of booty following a campaign. Caracalla doubled pay to 900 *denarii* but this put such a strain on Imperial finances and when Macrinus and Severus Alexander attempted to reintroduce Septimius Severus' level, it caused disaffection and mutiny. When Maximinus

seized the throne in 235 he apparently doubled pay to 1,800 *denarii*. Inflation, however, was rife throughout the 3rd century and the rise may not have been as great as it first appears. Caracalla had introduced a new coin, the *antoninianus*, which had a face value of two *denarii* but only the silver content of about one and a half, and by the middle of the 3rd century the silver content dropped so dramatically that some *antoniniani* of Gallienus' reign (260–68) were merely base metal with a silver wash. With much of the coinage virtually worthless the soldiers came to rely on the donatives of bullion and rations (Speidel, M.A., 1992; Alston 1994).

Legionaries also received a lump sum pension at the end of service known as *praemia*, perhaps equivalent to ten or 12 years' pay.

ESSENTIAL ORGANISATION AND COMMAND

Throughout our period the legion was composed of ten cohorts. Cohorts II–X were built around six centuries each containing 80 men, making a cohort 480 men strong. Cohort I had only five centuries but these were of double size, making a complement of 800 legionaries. Uniquely, legio II Parthica had six centuries in its first cohort but it is uncertain if these were of double size. With an additional 120 cavalry the legion numbered 5,240 at maximum strength.

Panels on the Arch of Constantine finished in 315, reused from a triumphal monument of Marcus Aurelius constructed after 176. The second panel shows Marcus (his head replaced with Constantine's) addressing legionaries and praetorians. (Author's collection)

Centuries and centurions

A centurion commanded each century. The centuries in each cohort were organised in three pairs of *prior* (front) and *posterior* (rear), and classed as *pili*, *principes* or *hastati*. The *prior* centurion had seniority over the *posterior* centurion. *Pili* centurions were the most senior in the cohort, followed by *principes*, then by the *hastati*. No cohort had an overall commander; they were simply tactical groupings of centuries. In fact, the titles of Imperial centurions recalled the triple battle lines of the Republican legion:

1	*pilus prior* *pilus posterior*
2	*princeps prior* *princeps posterior*
3	*hastatus prior* *hastatus posterior*

This suggests that the centurial titles still retained their tactical meaning and were evident even in the early 4th century (e.g. *ILS* 2332). The six centuries of the cohort could form up six-deep in battle, the *posterior* centuries supporting the *prior* centuries. This was effectively a triple battle line, in which the second line of *principes* could relieve or reinforce the *pili* as necessary, and the third line of *hastati* act as a reserve or perform outflanking manoeuvres. More usually, the cohort would form up in a line of two centuries, *prior* backed by *posterior*. Such lines were not continuous. There were spaces between the centuries and substantial gaps between cohorts in battle lines for the cohesion of the individual units and to facilitate the advance of reinforcements to the front (Speidel, M.P., 1992a RL, 7–9, 46–50).

The only centurions of clear superior rank in the legion were those of the first cohort, known as the *primi ordines* (front rankers). There were only five *primi ordines*, there being no *pilus posterior*, except for the unique case of legio II Parthica (*AE* 1993: 1588). The *primus pilus* (meaning 'first spear/javelin') was the most senior of the *primi ordines*. This was the seldom-reached pinnacle of the centurion's career and the post was held for only one year. His century contained the *aquilifer*, the senior standard-bearer who carried the eagle standard (*aquila*) embodying the *genius* (spirit) of the legion, which was crucial to unit identity and morale. Despite the status of the *primus pilus* there is no evidence that he had overall command of the first cohort and by the end of the 3rd century he was actually detached from his command.

From 213 we hear of a tax named after the *primus pilus* that was connected with the supply of the army. Administering its collection was an increasingly important function of the chief centurion but he remained a fighting soldier until the early 250s.

In 253 Sattonius Iucundus was *primus pilus* of legio III Augusta. The legion was disbanded in 238/9 for its support of Maximinus against the Gordians, but when this happened Iucundus was serving with a detachment of the legion in Europe and for the next 14 or 15 years his stranded unit fought Germans and Goths. The legion was re-formed in 253 with Iucundus as its first *primus pilus*. On his retirement Iucundus dedicated a statue 'to the most powerful god of war' – a reference to the extensive warfare he had seen. He also laid his *vitis* – the centurion's vine stick and ancient badge of rank – to rest in the shrine of the eagle

(*ILS* 2296). Within a few years Iucundus' successors in III Augusta were principally concerned with the maintenance of the legion's supplies and by 286 the rank of *primus pilus* had become hereditary so that it passed to sons who were not even soldiers. With the passing of the *primus pilus* as a command officer the *primi ordines* also ceased to exist and cohort I was no different from cohorts X–II (Cooper 1968: 290–93). Thus Iucundus' dedication of his vine stick in 253 attains the poignancy of an ancient military caste saying farewell.

The centurion was supported by a number of under-officers. The *signifer* (standard-bearer) carried the standard the soldiers followed into battle, relaying visual orders and acting as a rallying point. The *optio* was the centurion's deputy, who in battle maintained order from behind, using a staff to shove soldiers back into line, and would assume command if the centurion was killed. The *cornicen* or *bucinator* (trumpeter) would relay commands from the general to the century. The *tesserarius* (officer of the watchword) was concerned with guard duties and aided the *optio* in battle.

The centurion fought at the front and always figured highly in the casualties:

> To the Spirits of the Departed. Gratius Artilleus [and] Clodius Glamosus, centurions of legio VIII Augusta, killed in the Serdican War. The schola [association] of centurions of the above named legion [made this] for their well-deserving colleagues. (Šašel 1961: 4)

Artilleus and Glamosus were serving in the field army of Gallienus when it met and defeated the forces of the usurper Fulvius Macrianus near Serdica (Sofia, Bulgaria) in 261. The unusual outcome of the battle highlights the essential function and influence of the standard-bearers over the soldiers:

> And so the emperor [Gallienus] sent Aureolus, with other generals too, against Macrinus [the elder Macrianus] and his son Macrianus. And when they met in battle, they surrounded them and killed some; they spared others as family, and they hoped that those spared would go over to the emperor. However, they did not give way at first; but everyone went over to the emperor because of a bit of bad luck. For, as they were going, the men around the commanders held their standards straight; but one of those carrying the standards became entangled and fell as they were marching, and his standard was brought down. And all those remaining who were carrying standards saw the lowered standard and did not know why it was lowered; they assumed that the man holding it had dipped it deliberately, changing sides to the emperor [Gallienus]. And straightaway they too dropped all the standards and dashed them to the ground and acclaimed Gallienus, with the Pannonians

Legionary *antoninianus* of Gallienus, commemorating the role of legio VIII Augusta in his field army. The coin shows the legion's bull emblem. (Hunter Coin Cabinet, University of Glasgow)

the only ones left with Macrinus. Then when they too wished to change sides, Macrinus required that they should not surrender them, but kill them first and in this way go to the emperor. And having done this, the Pannonians handed themselves over. (Zonaras, 12.24, translated by Kathleen McLaughlin)

The third essential under-officer was the *optio*. If the centurion was killed or incapacitated he would leave his position at the rear of the century and assume command. The *tesserarius* was then solely responsible for keeping the rear ranks in order and shoving back-stepping soldiers into line with his staff. In assuming command the *optio* became a focus for enemy attack and the casualty rates among *optiones* were accordingly high. The gravestone of Aelius Septimus, *optio* of legio I Adiutrix, records that he was killed in battle, but the name of the enemy is lost (*CIL* III, 4310). However, the gravestone has a relief showing Septimus in battle fighting on the exposed right of the battle line, with sword drawn and shield raised high, barbarians falling before him, suggesting that he was killed having taken command of the century (Mócsy 1974, pl. 12b)

Cavalry and the *comitatus*

The legion also had 120 cavalry (*equites*) who acted as a bodyguard to the commander as well as messengers and scouts. The number of troopers per legion may have increased during the 3rd century and during the sole reign of Gallienus (260–68), many were detached to form elite cavalry units called *promoti* in his *comitatus*.

The *comitatus* was a mobile field army under the emperor's direct command with the praetorians, elements of legio II Parthica and other guard units at its core. Gallienus added units detached from the legions, forming an essential central reserve that was not bound to frontier defence and could be rapidly deployed to counter invaders and usurpers.

Praefectus legionis

From the beginning of our period until about 260, most legions were commanded by a senatorial officer, the legate (*legatus*) (*RL*, 8). Legio II Traiana, based near Alexandria, differed in being commanded by a prefect (*praefectus*), a former *primus pilus* who had been promoted to the equestrian order. All three Parthian legions were also under the command of equestrian prefects, professional soldiers such as Licinius Hierocletus, who commanded legio II Parthica early in the reign of Severus Alexander (before 227). Before his promotion to II Parthica he had been *primus pilus* twice, commanded one of the urban cohorts (the militarised police of Rome), and led an elite auxiliary unit of Mauretanian infantry with cavalry against the Parthians in 216–18 (*ILS* 1356). One of his predecessors, Aelius Triccianus, had joined one of the Pannonian legions (I & II Adiutrix, X & XIV Gemina) as a common soldier, was promoted to the staff of a provincial governor and ultimately rose to command II Parthica against the Parthians in 216–17 (Dio, 78.13.3–4).

Between 260 and 268 Gallienus issued an edict banning senators from military commands (Aurelius Victor, *De Caesaribus*, 33), and by the end of the third century all legions were commanded by professional prefects.

Tribunes

Until the middle of the 3rd century the legate or prefect had six tribunes on his staff who outranked the centurions but were normally concerned with administration and held no permanent command over the cohorts. The legate had one *tribunus laticlavius* ('broad stripe tribune' – a reference to senatorial insignia), who was still in his teens or early twenties, and after this post would enter the Senate and embark on a mixed civil service and military career. His class meant that he outranked the remaining five tribunes of equestrian rank (*tribuni angusticlavii* – 'narrow stripes') despite the fact that they were mature men and had held commands over auxiliary units. Legions commanded by *praefecti* presumably had six equestrian tribunes.

Only in times of war did the tribune hold any tactical command over the legionaries (Arrian, *Ectaxis Contra Alanos*, 5–6, 24), and their administrative staff resumed their fighting duties:

> Aurelius Veteranus beneficiarius [clerk] of the laticlavius (tribune) of legio XIII Gemina, killed in the battle line, who lived 26 years, 7 months, 15 days. Aurelius Secundianus, imaginifer [standard-bearer] of the above named legion, had this Memorial made for his well-deserving cousin. (*ILS* 2406)

Legionary *antoninianus* of Gallienus (c.259/60), commemorating legio XIII Gemina. These coins were issued to the legionary vexillations serving with Gallienus in northern Italy and celebrate three major victories. (Hunter Coin Cabinet, University of Glasgow)

The gravestone was discovered at Tortona in north-west Italy and the battle in which Veteranus died may be connected with one of the many barbarian incursions or civil wars of the mid-3rd century. The inscription is notable because it may be one of the latest references to the senatorial tribune and because it shows that even the legion's administrative staff took their place in the battle line.

Gallienus' edict would have abolished the rank of senatorial tribune but the equestrian tribune also fades from view at this time to be replaced with *praepositi* risen from the ranks.

Vexillations

Complete legions still took the field under Marcus Aurelius and occasionally thereafter but by the middle of the 3rd century it was extremely rare for a full legion to leave its provincial base to fight abroad. For the duration of Lucius Verus' Parthian War (162–66) three legions – I Minervia, II Adiutrix and V Macedonica – were transferred from Europe to the East, but in the subsequent wars against the Germans and Sarmatians (168–80) many legions were deployed not as complete bodies but in detachments called *vexillationes*, so called because they marched under banners called *vexilla*. Already in 170 Marcus Aurelius' recently established legions II and III Italica were operating in vexillations (a term that could be applied to any size of detachment or work party). An inscription from Solin in Croatia records detachments from the legions (using their original titles *Pia* ('loyal') and *Concordia* ('united')) fortifying the ancient city of Salonae to protect it from barbarian incursions during the Marcomannic War. Interestingly, a senior intelligence officer (*centurio frumentarius*) from another legion oversaw the construction:

> To the Emperor Caesar Marcus Aurelius Antoninus Augustus, chief priest, in the twenty-fourth year of his tribunician power, consul for the third time, vexillations of legions II Pia and III

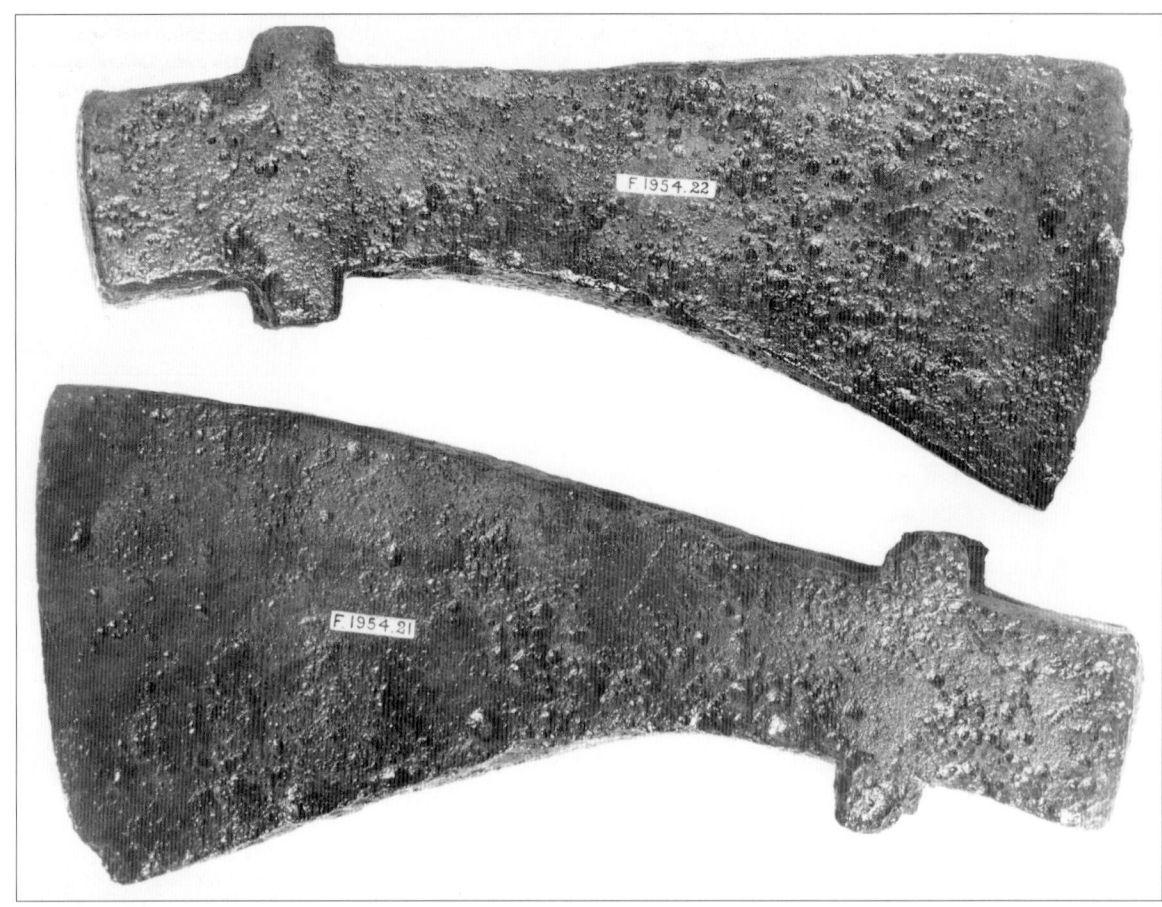

Roman military axes from Loudoun Hill, Scotland, 1st–2nd century. The legions excelled in construction and in peacetime would often work on civil projects. (Hunterian Museum, University of Glasgow)

Concordia [built] 200 feet [of wall] under the direction of Publius Aelius Amyntianus, *centurio frumentarius* of legio II Traiana. (*ILS* 2287)

Complete legions did fight in the wars of Septimius Severus and Caracalla – a notable example is II Traiana in 213 when it won the title *Germanica* for a victory over the Cenni – but increasingly their field armies were composed of vexillations. Thereafter the legion became a kind of static reserve, sending out detachments from its base as necessary for field or garrison service without compromising its responsibilities for frontier defence and provincial policing. The tactical situation faced by the Empire in the later 2nd and 3rd centuries was better served by vexillations that could be moved more easily in terms of speed and logistics than complete legions. Massed in appropriate numbers, vexillations could tackle large armies, or be dispersed to combat less numerous opponents. They also provided strong garrisons for the protection of important road junctions, passes and river crossings. This was a logical progression of a practice evident from the establishment of the Imperial legions, and we should recall that the legion was never really a tactical organisation – it was simply too large – but an administrative organisation: the cohorts and centuries were always the tactical bodies.

Combat vexillations were normally composed of one or two cohorts. These retained their regular centurial organisation and would fight as

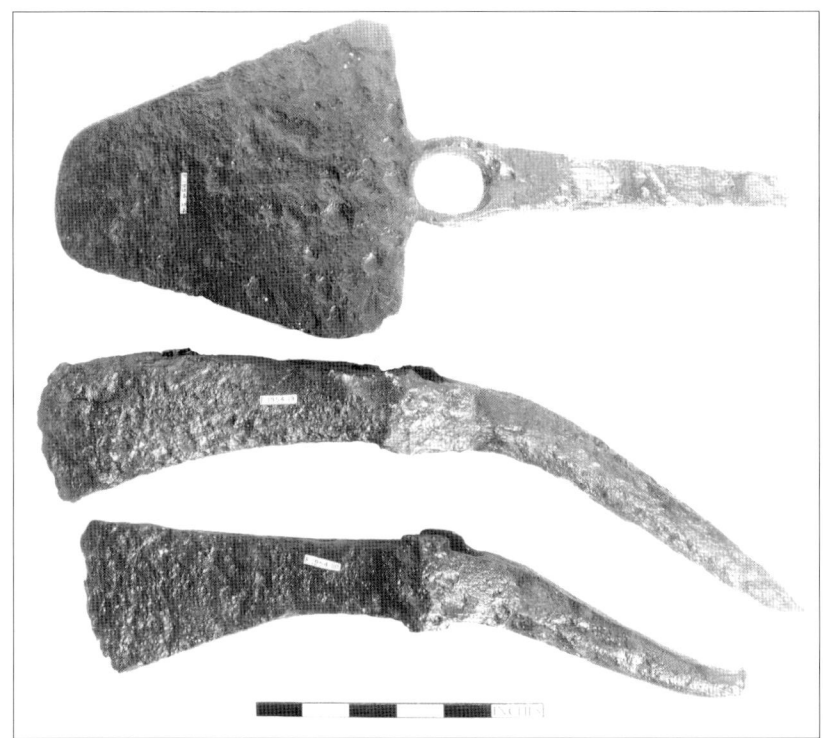

groups of *centuriae* in the field, for the vexillation was effectively a legion in miniature. With additional administrative and logistical staff, such detachments numbered *c*.500 (one cohort = *quingenaria*) or 1,000 men (two cohorts = *milliaria*), and were commanded by an officer with the title of *praepositus* (Saxer 1967).

In the early 3rd century a vexillation performing garrison duty at an outlying fort might expect to stay there for up to three years, but field service could last much longer. Some of the units participating in the Parthian War of 216–18 had marched east in 214 and only returned home between 219 and 221. In the endemic warfare of the later 3rd century some vexillations were in the field for so long that they effectively became independent, and those that survived were ultimately organised into mini-legions carrying the

numerals and names of their parent legions. For example, in the 4th century the old legio III Italica existed as five frontier legions in the province of Raetia and a sixth elite legion serving in the mobile field army (*comitatenses*) of Illyricum (Notitia Dignitatum, *Occidentis*, 35.17–19, 21, 22; 5.237).

The last traditionally organised Roman legion to fight as a complete unit was probably legio II Parthica, in the Persian war of Gordian III (242–44). This was because the legion was based in central Italy and consequently had no sector of frontier to defend. Its creator, Septimius Severus, envisaged that the legion be reserved for use as a complete unit

Bronze roundel, commemorating the vexillations of legions XX Valeria Victrix and II Augusta, probably operating together as a combined unit of *c*.1,000 men under the command of Aurelius Cervianus, perhaps *c*.253–68. Of uncertain provenance, found somewhere in France. (Drawn by Steven D.P. Richardson)

and, along with the 10,000-strong Praetorian Guard, it formed the core of all Imperial expeditionary forces, but by *c*.260 even II Parthica operated in *vexillationes*. From 257/8 detachments of II Parthica served in the *comitatus* against the Alamanni in Germany and Italy (Cooper 1968: 266ff), and later we find a vexillation of II Parthica and a detachment from the recently restored legio III Augusta guarding a strategically important road in Macedonia against the Goths, *c*.260–68 (*AE* 1934: 193).

Wives and concubines

The increasing use of vexillations was also influenced by another significant factor – the wives and families of the soldiers. At the start of our period the legions were firmly established in their provincial bases. Soldiers were recruited locally and they formed relationships with local women. Settlements called *canabae* grew up around the legionary fortresses, originally to cater for the needs of the soldiers – shops, taverns, brothels – but soon expanded to include the homes of the soldiers' dependants. Legionaries were loath to leave their homes and families to fight abroad and the use of vexillations limited the number of soldiers who would have to leave family and home for a number of years. However, as we have seen, some complete legions did go to war during the first half of the 3rd century, and the concerns for faraway wives and children led to discord and mutiny.

The emperor Augustus (27 BC to AD 14) banned legionaries from contracting legal marriages until they were discharged from service.

This may have been an attempt to limit the number of non-combatants attached to the legion and prevent soldiers from becoming too tied to a particular area in case military exigency demanded that they be rapidly and permanently transferred elsewhere. Tacitus said that legionaries 'lacked the habit of marrying wives and rearing children' (*Annals*, 14.27), but it is clear that they had done both even during Augustus' reign. For example, when in AD 9 Varus' army of three legions and auxiliaries was ambushed and destroyed in the Teutoburg Forest by the Cherusci, a powerful German tribe. The historian Dio observed disapprovingly that the Roman field army was accompanied by substantial numbers of women and children, but he noted with respect that the legionaries who had been left to garrison forts made desperate attempts to save their women and children when attacked by the Cherusci (Dio, 66.20.2, 22.2–4).

It was not until 197 that the ban on marriage was officially lifted. Having defeated his rival Clodius Albinus at Lugdunum, Septimius Severus rewarded his troops with increased pay, better prospects of promotion, and recognised their right to marry (Herodian, 3.8.4–5). However, the Severan emperors clearly made attempts to limit the numbers of women and children accompanying armies on campaign. If we examine the gravestones of soldiers of legio II Parthica who died whilst the legion was fighting in the Middle East between 216 and 244, we find that ordinary legionaries were commemorated by comrades but some centurions and senior 'under-officers' were buried by their wives. For example:

> To Antonia Cara, who lived 28 years and 4 months, Probius Sanctus centurion of legio II Parthica had this made for his incomparable and well deserving wife. (Apamea, *AE* 1993: 1597)

Another poignant gravestone from Turkey records how Flavius Maritimus, centurion of II Parthica, buried his three-month-old son at Cnidus in the province of Asia (Turkey) on 27 September 244 (*CIL* III, 14403a). The date indicates that the legion was marching back to Europe having fought in the ultimately disastrous war against the Persians (below).

These and other inscriptions reveal that wives and children accompanied centurions and their senior under-officers, such as eagle-bearers and *optiones*, to and from the regions close to where the fighting was, but no legionary below the rank of *tesserarius* is commemorated by a wife (see Balty & Van Rengen 1993). The clear implication is that ordinary legionaries were not permitted to take their wives abroad. They seem to have accepted this up to a point and were resigned to the fact that they might be thousands of miles from home for several years, but they demanded that their families be protected whilst they were away. In 233 Severus Alexander was wintering with the field army at Antioch in Syria having fought the Persians with mixed success in Mesopotamia and Media. When news arrived that the Alamanni had overrun the frontiers of Noricum, Raetia and upper Germany, the soldiers transferred from those provinces for the war in the East turned their anger on the emperor:

> They felt they had suffered a double tragedy, first in their misfortunes in the Persian war and then in the reports they received individually about the destruction of their families by the Germans. They turned their anger on Alexander, blaming him for the betrayal of their cause in the East through his negligence or cowardice and his hesitant procrastination over the northern crisis. (Herodian, 6.7.3, after Whittaker 1969–70)

Archaeology confirms the violent destruction of many auxiliary forts in Germany at this time, though it has been suggested that some were actually assaulted by other Romans in 235. By 234 Alexander had marched north and entered into peace negotiations with the Alamanni but this angered many soldiers and in March 235 Alexander was murdered and Maximinus, his prefect of recruits, was made emperor. Maximinus crushed the Alamanni in battle but he was not universally popular with the army and elements revolted, perhaps including legio VIII Augusta whose fortress at Strasbourg Maximinus may have been besieged and stormed. The destruction of some auxiliary forts may also have resulted from Roman versus Roman conflict rather than Barbarian incursion (Okamura 1996).

By spring 238 Maximinus had fought successfully against the Germans, Sarmatians and Carpi, and was preparing to campaign against the Goths from his base in Pannonia, but his wars were expensive and the province of Africa rebelled over brutal tax collection, setting up its governor Gordian and his son as emperors. The younger Gordian was soon killed in battle against legio III Augusta outside Carthage. At the prospect of facing the charge of the experienced soldiers his untrained levies 'threw away their equipment and ran without waiting for the charge. Pushing and trampling each other, more were killed by their own side than by the enemy' (Herodian, 7.9.7). The elder Gordian committed suicide. The Senate in Rome had declared for Gordian against the hated soldier emperor Maximinus, and proceeded with their rebellion even when the Gordians were defeated. The Senate elected two emperors from its own ranks, Pupienus and Balbinus, and arranged the defence of Italy. Having made a difficult crossing of the still wintry Alps, Maximinus determined to storm the northern city of Aquileia, which was manned by senatorial forces, and march on Rome. However, Maximinus' soldiers proved unable to storm the walls and ran short of supplies during the ensuing siege. Morale plummeted

Sestertius issued by Maximinus to celebrate his northern victories, 236–37. Maximinus and his son, Maximus, hold a small statue of Victory over bound barbarian captives. The soldier to the right holds a cylindrical *scutum*. (Hunter Coin Cabinet, University of Glasgow)

and the legionaries of II Parthica, whose wives and children in Albanum were effectively the hostages of the Senate, decided to act before their families were harmed:

> Maximinus was resting in his quarters during a break in the fighting … Most of the soldiers had also retired to their tents or to the guard post allotted to their charge. Suddenly the soldiers from the camp on Mount Alba near Rome (where they had left behind wives and children) decided to murder Maximinus, so that they could abandon the endless siege … With great daring the soldiers went to Maximinus' tent at about midday and, with the help of the praetorians, tore his image from the standards. When Maximinus and his son came out of their tent and attempted to reason with the soldiers, they were killed without being heard. The praetorian prefect was also killed, as were all of Maximinus' close advisors. Their bodies were thrown out for anyone to desecrate or trample, before being left to be torn to pieces by dogs and birds. The heads of Maximinus and his son were sent to Rome. (Herodian, 8.5.8–9, after Whittaker 1969–70)

Legionary *antoninianus* of Gallienus (c.259/60), showing one of legio I Italica's emblems, here a boar. (Hunter Coin Cabinet, University of Glasgow)

The assassination of Maximinus illustrates the lengths to which legionaries were prepared to go to protect their wives and children. However, there was a darker side to soldiers' relationships with women. A substantial number of soldiers' 'wives' were in fact slaves bought to act as servants and concubines. A Roman master could freely have sex with his slave without her consent, and the slave had no recourse if subjected to other physical abuse. It was even within the bounds of law for a Roman to kill his slave. However, it is clear from inscriptions that many female slaves were granted their freedom and remained attached to their former masters (though we should not discount dependency as a factor).

The army actually kept female slaves as prostitutes for the entertainment of its soldiers. Evidence from Dura-Europos suggests that soldiers had free use of military prostitutes and that they were rotated around brothels attached to military installations in Syria (Pollard 2000: 53–4, 188). The risk of sexual disease and the dangers of abortion and childbirth must have limited their life expectancy considerably.

ELITE LEGIONARIES

Most legionaries were heavy infantrymen who fought in close order with sword and heavy javelin (*pilum*), but the legions had always contained specialist fighters. However, it was not until the early 3rd century that such legionaries were recognised with official ranks (or titles), and for most of the century they are attested in only one legion – II Parthica.

Lanciarii

Since 1879 regular finds of inscriptions from Apamea in Syria have revealed much important and unique information about the organisation of legio II Parthica. During the Parthian and Persian wars of Caracalla, Severus Alexander and Gordian III, the legion had its winter quarters at Apamea and its periodic stays left a wealth of epigraphic evidence (Balty & Van Rengen 1993). After the city was sacked by Shapur I of Persia in the 250s, a large number of gravestones commemorating soldiers of II Parthica were used to reinforce the city walls, particularly in tower XV, where more than 130 inscriptions have been discovered. As well as attesting the presence of the legion at Apamea at various periods, the inscriptions have revealed a number of new ranks unique to the legion. Primary among them is that of *lanciarius*.

The *lanciarii* of legio II Parthica are recorded on three gravestones dating to Caracalla's and Macrinus' Parthian War, 215–18. The stones bear portraits of the dead, showing them holding bundles of four or five small *lanceae*, the light javelins from which they drew their title of 'lancer' (*AE* 1993: 1573–75). The light javelins indicate that the legion's *lanciarii* could act as open-order skirmishers like the ancient *velites*, fighting before the main battle line of heavy infantry or protecting the gaps between the cohorts and vexillations from infiltration by the enemy. Some of the troops who performed this function at the Battle of Nisibis in 217 were almost certainly *lanciarii*:

> With loud shrieks and yells the [Parthians] charged the Romans, with [horse] archers firing and cavalry at the gallop. But the disposition of the Roman units was orderly and careful. With cavalry and Moorish soldiers on either flank, *and the spaces in the centre* [the gaps between the units of heavy infantry] *were filled with light armed troops capable of making marauding forays.* So they sustained the attack and fought back. The barbarians inflicted heavy casualties with their showers of arrows and with the lances of the cataphracts [heavily armoured cavalry] mounted on horses and camels, as they wounded the Romans with downward thrusts. But the Romans easily had the better of those who came to hand-to-hand combat. When the numbers of cavalry and camels began to cause them trouble, they feigned a retreat and threw down caltrops and other iron traps with sharp spikes sticking out of them. These were deadly to the cavalry and camels because they lay hidden in the sand and were not seen. The horses and camels trod on them, particularly the camels with their soft pads, and fell to their knees and were lamed, throwing their riders from their backs. (Herodian, 4.15.1–3, after Whittaker 1969–70)

Lanciarii could also be drawn up behind the heavy infantry to supply missile support over the heads of their comrades (Arrian, *Ectaxis Contra Alanos*, 15–18, 25–26; cf. Dio 74.7.2).

Early *lanciarii*

The *lanciarii* of legio II Parthica are the first attested in any legion but are not the earliest known in the Imperial army. That honour goes to troopers of the ala Sebosiana, a cavalry unit based in Britain in the late 1st century

AD. In a letter to the unit's commander the officer Docilis gives the names of the *lanciarii* within his *turma* (troop of 30 cavalry) 'who were missing lances'. Docilis' letter reveals that his mounted *lanciarii* were armed with two types of *lancea*: a single heavy thrusting weapon, a lance or pike as the modern reader would understand it; and two *lanceae subarmales*, smaller throwing javelins (Tomlin 1999). The *lanciarii* of II Parthica were clearly armed with the latter weapon.

Although the *lanciarii* of II Parthica are the first legionaries to bear the rank, lightly armed troops had always been part of the legion's make-up. A mid-to-late 1st century sculpture on a column base from the legionary headquarters building at Mainz shows a lightly equipped legionary armed with three short javelins and an oval shield

Legionary *antoninianus* of Gallienus (c.259/60), showing one of legio I Italica's emblems, here a hippocampus ('sea horse'). (Hunter Coin Cabinet, University of Glasgow)

(*RL*, 26). The other column bases show heavily armed legionaries with rectangular *scuta* and *pila* fighting in close order (*RL*, 31), but the lightly armed legionary runs forward alone, indicating that he is skirmishing in front of the line of heavy infantry. Also discovered at Mainz was the gravestone of Flavoleius Cordus of legio XIV Gemina dating to before AD 43. Cordus is portrayed with a long slender javelin with a throwing thong to increase range and a large oval shield instead of the regular *scutum*. These should identify him as a dedicated skirmisher, for the oval shield was more suited to fighting in open ranks (*RL*, 31).

Tacitus suggests the use of the *lancea* by legionaries of III Gallica in his description of the destruction of a force of Rhoxolani in 69 (Histories, 1.79). Nearer to our period, in 135, half of the soldiers of the Cappadocian legions, XII Fulminata and XV Apollinaris, were armed with *pila*, the other half with lanceae, for battle against the heavy cavalry of the Alani (Arrian, *Ectaxis contra Alanos*, 15–18). The division of arms may only have resulted for the particular tactics devised for the battle: a continuous and stationary battle line in which the first four ranks of legionaries used their *pila* to present a wall of spikes to the charging Alani, whilst the rear four ranks bombarded them with *lanceae*. However, the armament may have been standard for when the satirist Lucian was given a pair of guards from the same legions to escort him whilst on official duties in the 160s, he notes that one soldier was armed with a 'pike' (probably a *pilum*), the other with a *lancea* (Lucian, *Alexander*, 55).

Most interestingly, Dio describes how in 185 an angry 'delegation' of 1,500 legionaries from Britain was permitted by Commodus to lynch the increasingly powerful praetorian prefect Perennis, whom they believed to be plotting against the emperor. Dio describes the soldiers as javelin men (Dio, 72.9.2–3). Their selection for the 'delegation' by the legates of Britain suggests that they were the elite troops of their legions, and their number indicates that each legion had at least 500 such troops, equivalent to the strength of a cohort. The legionaries may actually have belonged to three vexillations operating against deserters led by Maternus in Gaul, hence their easy march on Rome, but Dio's tale should allow us to view the *lanciarii* of II Parthica as elite troops within the legion, numbering perhaps 500 men. Finally, an inscription recording the dedication of a shield and *lancea* by a centurion of legio III Cyrenaica to the god Vihansa, shows that centurions could be similarly equipped and would lead skirmishers or direct the missile support from the rear ranks of the battle line (*ILS*, 4755).

Lanciarii and the sacred retinue

After their appearance at Apamea in 215–18 legionary *lanciarii* are not heard of again until the late 3rd century. We know of mounted *lanciarii* in Diocletian's new legio I Iovia Scythica (after 285; *AE* 1981: 777) and in 300 we find a vexillation of *lanciarii* from legio II Traiana and the *lanciarii* of legio III Diocletiana in Egypt (P. Beatty Panop. II, 285–7, 301). Funerary inscriptions also record a distinct unit of *lanciarii* from which soldiers were promoted to the Praetorian Guard in the late 3rd and early 4th centuries:

> To the Spirits of the Departed. Valerius Tertius, soldier of the tenth praetorian cohort, lived 36 years, three months, 15 days. He served in a Moesian legion for 5 years, in the *lanciarii* for 11 years, in the praetorians for [–] years in the century of Salvius. (*ILS*, 2045) Marcella had this made for Martinus, her well deserving husband, who lived 38 years. He served in [legio] I Minerva for 11 years, in [legio] IX [Claudia] for 4 years, in the *lanciarii* for 4 years, in the praetorians for 5 years. (*ILS*, 2782)

Tertius and Martinus entered a distinct unit of *lanciarii* from a Moesian legion (IV Flavia, VII Claudia, I Italica and XI Claudia), perhaps from the vexillations based at Aquileia in north-east Italy in the late 3rd to early 4th centuries (Speidel, M.P., 1990). The unit of *lanciarii* to which they were promoted was not a specialist legionary detachment but a new Guards unit created in the second half of the 3rd century:

> To the Spirits of the Departed. Valerius Thiumpus who served in legio XI Claudia, was selected as a lanciarius in the sacred retinue (sacer comitatus), then served as a protector for 5 years, discharged, was prefect of legio II Herculia for 2 years, 6 months and died aged 45. (*ILS*, 2781)

Thiumpus, who also originally served in a Moesian legion, was promoted to the *lanciarii* of the *sacer comitatus* ('sacred retinue', i.e. the personal field army of Diocletian or one of his immediate predecessors). Later Thiumpus was promoted to *protector*, a guard of the emperor equating in rank to a chief centurion and marked out for promotion to senior commands. Following his honourable discharge Thiumpus

Gold *aureus* issued by the Gallic emperor Victorinus, AD 268-70, and indicating that he had a vexillation of legio XIII Gemina in his army. The coin depicts the legion's lion emblem. (Hunter Coin Cabinet, University of Glasgow)

was made commander of Diocletian's new legion II Herculia. Tertius and Martinus were promoted to the same elite unit of *lanciarii* as Thiumpus, to *the Lanciarii*, not the *lanciarii* within or derived from a particular legion. They also were part of the sacred retinue, allowing them to be promoted to its most senior unit, the Praetorian Guard.

It is probable that this unit of *lanciarii* had its origin in legio II Parthica. In 260 Gallienus set about making his field army a permanent institution and from this time II Parthica was finally deployed in vexillations (see Vexillations, above) and it is tempting to see the *lanciarii* being formally detached from the legion during this period. Thus elevated to a status above the legions and just below the Praetorian Guard in seniority, the *lanciarii* survived their parent legion and formed the core of the palatine legions of *lanciarii*, the most senior in the late Roman Army (*lanciarii seniores* and *iuniores*: Notitia Dignitatum, *Orientis*, 5.2 = 42, 6.7 = 47).

Phalangarii

Dio records that the emperor Caracalla raised a phalanx of 15,000 recruited from Macedonia and equipped in the ancient fashion with pike and linen cuirass (Dio, 77.7.1–2). This unit and a further phalanx of Spartans is also reported by Herodian (4.8.2–3, 9–4). However, surviving gravestones of the Spartan phalangites indicate that their 'phalanx' was in reality a standard cohort of 500–1,000 soldiers, and that the soldiers were equipped similarly to the legionaries with regular oval shields, medium-length swords and even cuirasses of *lorica segmentata* (e.g. *ILS*, 8878). This suggests a combination with other regular Roman heavy infantry equipment and consequently the normal function and tactics of the legionary or auxiliary. The real identity and function of Dio's 'Macedonian phalanx' is easily solved. Caracalla was embarking on a war against Parthia and wished to emulate the successes of Alexander the Great (336–323 BC) who had conquered an immense territory stretching from Turkey to northern India. Caracalla consequently formed his own Macedonian phalanx. The 'Macedonians' were probably praetorians and legionaries of II Parthica. A number of these soldiers did originate in Macedonia but mostly from neighbouring Thrace; indeed the units drew most of their recruits from this region. The praetorians numbered 10,000 and II Parthica about 5,000, thus supplying the total figure of 15,000. Their pikes either refer to thrusting

Gravestone of Aurelius Alexianus, a soldier from Sparta who served in Caracalla's Spartan cohort, *c.*212–17. He probably wears *lorica segmentata*. His club is an attribute of Hercules but may also represent the soldier's *fustis*. He wears the traditional Spartan *pilos* cap. Now in the National Archaeological Museum, Athens. (Drawn by Steven D.P. Richardson)

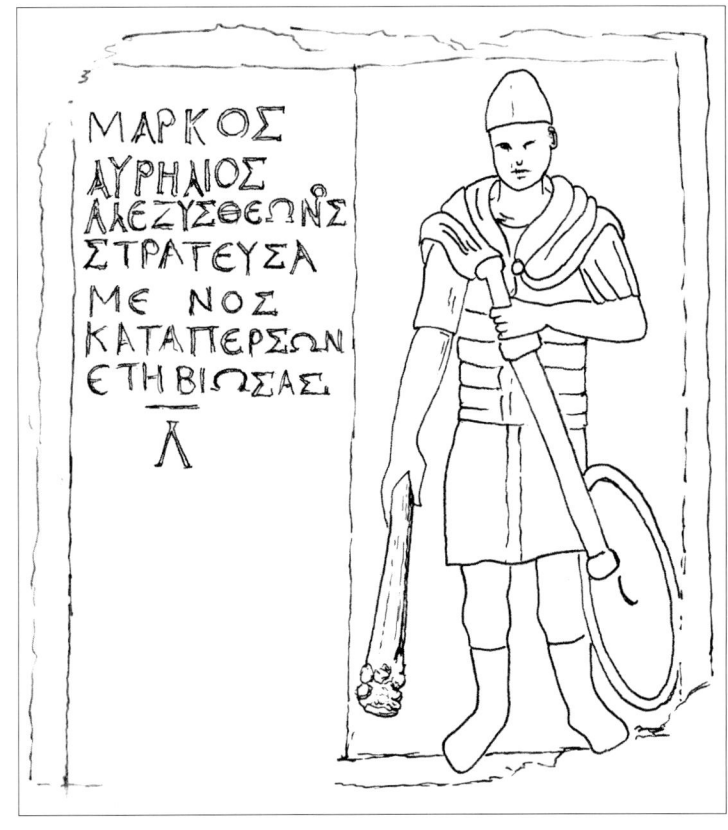

spears with which some Roman soldiers had always been equipped, or to *pila*. Arrian stated that his legionaries were equipped with pikes in 131 but his description, 'pikes that end in long, slender points', recalls the long iron shank of the *pilum* (*Ectaxis Contra Alanos*, 16). The linen cuirass could be correct, a special light armour designed for the heat of the Middle East, but it could also apply to the *thoracomachus* or *subarmilis*, the padded linen garment worn beneath armour to absorb the shock of blows and sometimes worn as defence by itself (Dio, 77.7.2, 78.3.2). Dio also records that he watched Caracalla drill the Macedonian phalanx at Nicomedia (Turkey) in 214, but he simply distorts the standard training of household troops in advance of a major campaign; Severus Alexander did exactly the same in 231 (Dio, 77.18.1; Herodian, 6.3.3).

Severus Alexander also had a 'Macedonian Phalanx' that served with success in his Persian War (231–33). We even know of a legionary of II Parthica who served in this war and was described on his gravestone as a *phalangarius* (inscription unpublished, see Balty 1988), but he did not fight in an antiquated Macedonian phalanx-type unit at all:

> [Alexander] made every effort to ... surpass the Macedonian king. [He had] a phalanx of 30,000 men whom he ordered to be called phalangarii, and with these he won many victories in Persia. This phalanx ... was formed from six legions, and was armed like the other troops. (Historia Augusta, *Severus Alexander*, 50.4–5)

That the phalanx was formed from whole legions must be doubted – the only complete legion present in the field army was II Parthica – but it proves that the 'phalanx' was simply a title applied to regular units fighting in the East wishing to emulate the glorious victories of Alexander the Great.

Belief and belonging

Units that had supported the losing side in a civil war might be disbanded and suffer *damnatio memoriae*. This terrible punishment wiped a unit from the army lists and its name and numeral were erased from all monuments, eradicating any trace of its previous existence. Its soldiers were either dishonourably discharged or were ignominiously transferred to faraway units. This was an ultimate punishment for the unit in which he served defined a soldier's identity. Those who were dishonourably discharged were often reduced to brigandage to survive, while transfers to other units were probably ostracised lest their presence taint the esprit de corps of a loyal legion. The most notable example of our period is legio III Augusta, disbanded by Gordian III in 238–39 for its support of Maximinus and its role in the deaths of Gordian I and Gordian II (see above, Wives and concubines).

No account survives of III Augusta's dissolution, but we possess many details of the disbanding of the Praetorian Guard in 193 for the murder of the emperor Pertinax. Septimius. Severus' Pannonian legionaries surrounded the praetorians, who had been tricked into parading unarmed outside Rome, and 'rushed forward seizing from the praetorians their daggers which were inlaid with silver and gold ... and their belts ... and any other military insignia they were wearing' (Herodian, 2.13.10). The

Praetorian standard on the Arch of the Argentarii, Rome, 204. The standard carries images of Caracalla and Severus, but Geta's portrait was removed following his murder in 212. Below the images is a wall crown awarded for the capture of an enemy rampart. (Author's collection)

praetorians were thus stripped of their military identity and dishonourably discharged. Severus then had the standards of the Guard dragged through the streets of Rome, desecrating the sacred objects in which the *genii* (spirits) of the unit and its centuries resided (Historia Augusta, *Severus*, 7.1–2). Some praetorians committed suicide at the shame of it (Dio, 74.1). The dishonourable discharge of the praetorians allowed Severus to form a new Guard in which he enrolled the bravest of his Pannonian legionaries in reward for their crucial support.

Legio III Augusta was restored by Valerian and Gallienus in 253 to counter the increasing pressure from rebel tribes in Africa. At the core of legio III Augusta *restituta* (restored) was a vexillation that had been serving in Europe when the legion was disbanded. For 14 or 15 years this displaced and disgraced unit strove to maintain its independent identity even when they were added to the regional field army of Raetia and placed under the supervision of officers from legio III Italica (*ILS*, 2772). The now pseudo-legionaries swore to return to Africa and see their legion reborn. On 22 October 253 they fulfilled their vow (*ILS*, 531), and their determination is a clear illustration of their belief in the legion. It is probable that this vexillation marched with Valerian against Aemilianus in 253 and was suitably rewarded.

EQUIPMENT

Pilum

It has been suggested that the *pilum*, a heavy javelin up to 2m long with a long tapering iron shank and barbed head, ceased to be the principal weapon of the legionary in the 3rd century, with the thrusting spear and

Pedestal reliefs on the Arch of Constantine, 315. The first shows Roman soldiers leading barbarian captives; one soldier holds a light *pilum* or *spiculum*. The far base shows an *aquilifer* (eagle bearer) and *imaginifer* (a standard-bearer who carried the Imperial images). (Author's collection)

light javelins replacing it. However, the evidence is hardly conclusive. The *pilum* certainly disappears from the great triumphal monuments in Rome such as the Aurelian Column and the Arch of Severus, but the representation of equipment on these monuments is generally poor, and the sculptors found spears easier to depict.

Archaeology provides better evidence. *Pila* heads and shanks have been found in substantial numbers, particularly at legio II Augusta's fortress at Caerleon in Wales (dating to after 260) and the fort of Saalburg in Germany (*c.*260). More importantly, a *pilum* has been recovered from the battle debris at Krefeld-Gellep in Germany. This *pilum* was used to defend the fort of Gelduba from the Franks in *c.*275.

Light and heavy weighted *pila* are represented on the gravestones of legionaries and praetorians until the early 4th century and Ammianus reports legionaries using *spicula,* a form of socketed *pilum,* in battle against the Alamanni in 357 (Ammianus Marcellinus, 16.12.46). The *pilum* almost certainly remained the essential weapon of front-rank legionaries (Cowan 2002, chap. 4).

BELOW TOP **Gold *aureus* showing the emperor Probus (276–82) addressing the army from a tribunal. The soldiers hold standards and carry cylindrical scuta suggesting that this type of shield was still in use at the end of the 3rd century. (Hunter Coin Cabinet, University of Glasgow)**

BELOW BOTTOM **Unrestored and restored painted oval shield from Dura Europos, with war god motif, AD 256–57. (Dura-Europos Collection, Yale University Art Gallery)**

Shield

During our period most legionaries used flat or slightly dished, oval shields. Some were probably of laminate wood construction but finds from Dura-Europos (*c.*256–67) indicate that many were of simple plank construction, reinforced with iron bars and edged with stitched-on rawhide (Plate H). However, a traditional cylindrical *scutum* of triple laminate construction, faced with felt and leather, was also discovered at Dura and shows that the depiction of this shield on military coin types until the 280s was not anachronistic (Plate D).

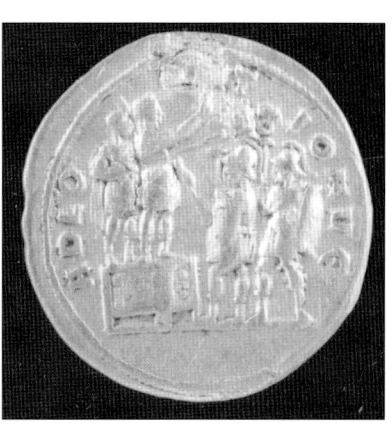

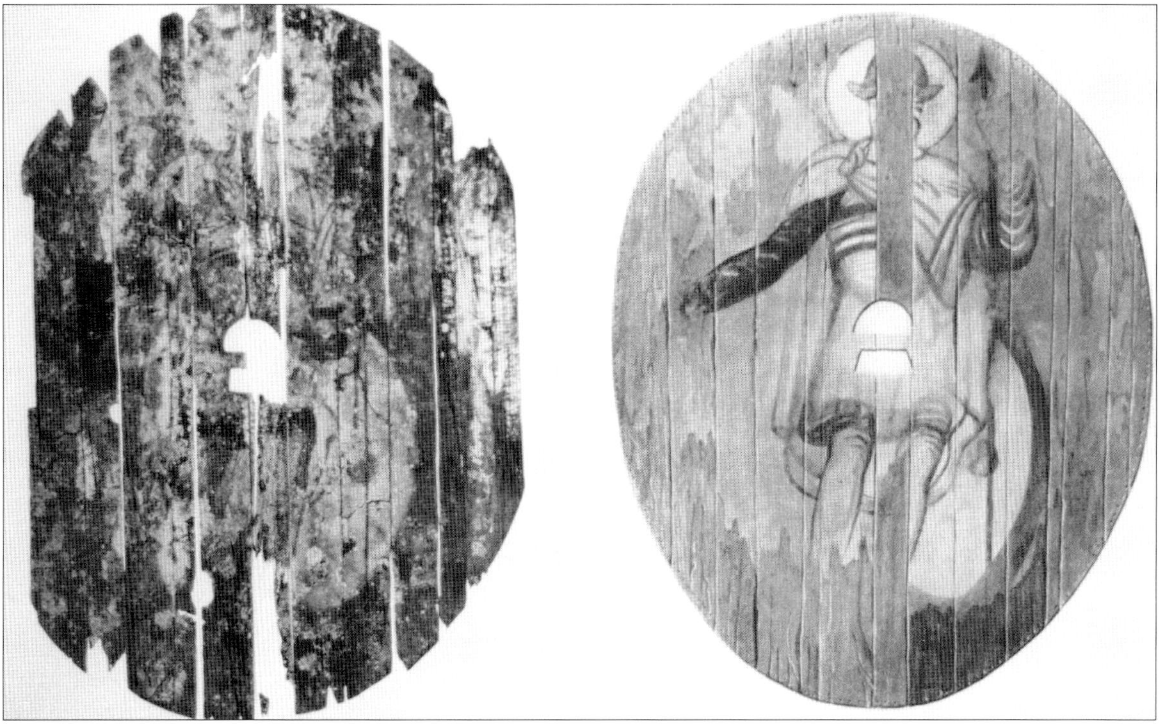

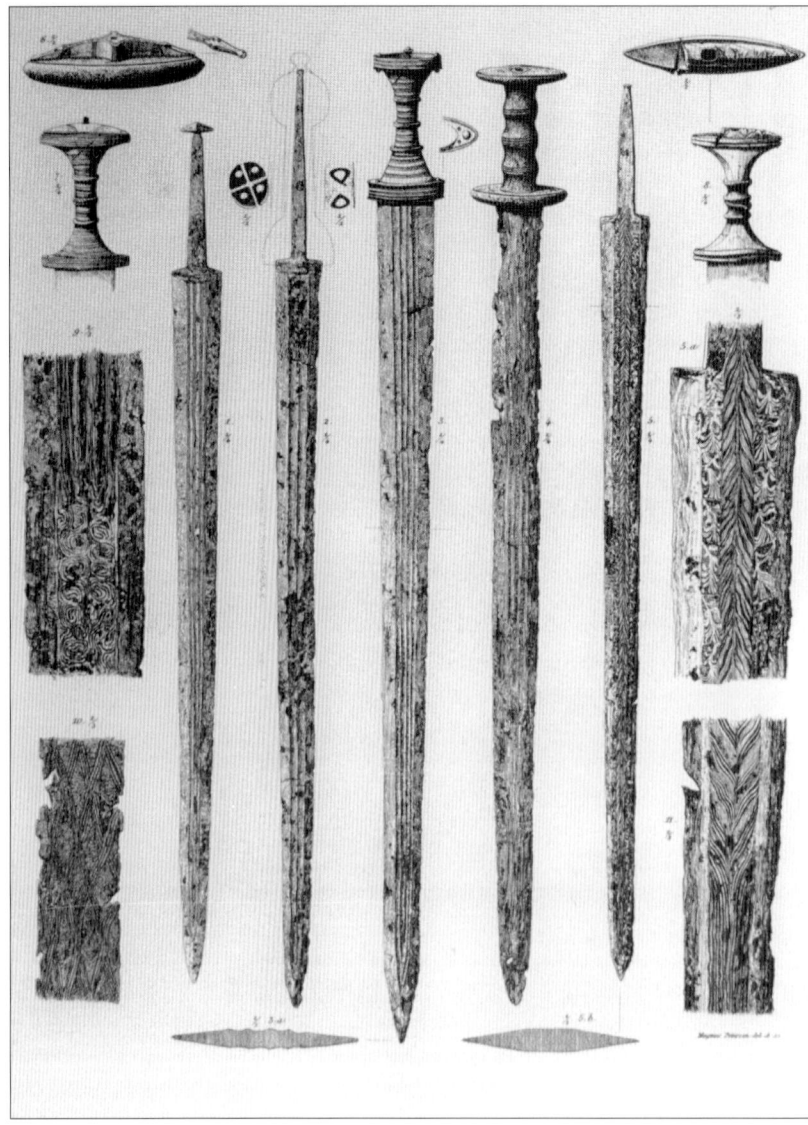

Sword

During the 2nd century Roman infantry generally ceased to use short swords and adopted medium-length and long swords. However, short swords did not disappear entirely, and most other swords were cut and thrust weapons with substantial triangular or tapering points, many of fine pattern-welded construction (Plate C). In fact, some of the longest Roman swords resemble the heavy rapiers of the early modern period, and should be considered as dedicated thrusting weapons. We have no evidence to suggest that the Roman fencing technique changed dramatically with the adoption of longer sword forms, i.e. that the sword was used to slash rather than thrust. In fact, our representational evidence continues to show soldiers in battle using swords to thrust, and Vegetius advocates the use of the sword point over the edge in his late 4th century account of legionary training (Vegetius, *Epitome*, 1.12). Ammianus confirms the issue when he states that legionaries used their swords to thrust at the Battle of Strasbourg in 357. Amid the crush and the shoving there was no room to use medium-length and long swords to slash, only to thrust and cut:

Roman swords of 3rd century date from Nydam, Denmark. From Engelhardt 1865.

> [The advancing Alamanni nobles] got as far as the legio Primanorum, which was positioned in the centre, in 'praetorian camp' formation. There our soldiers, in close order and in fully manned ranks, held their ground steadfastly, like towers ... Being intent on avoiding wounds, they protected themselves like murmillos,* and with drawn swords thrust at the enemy's sides, left unprotected by their frenzied rage. (Ammianus Marcellinus, 16.12.49).
>
> (*Murmillos were heavily armoured gladiators who probably fought with their left leg leading, and body turned in profile to their opponent so as to present as small a target as possible.)

Legionaries mid-2nd century AD

A

B

Legionary centurion awarded with *torques* and *armillae* by Marcus Aurelius

Roman pattern welded swords, 3rd century AD

C

Archery practice

Maximinus as *dux ripae* with his bodyguards, Dura-Europos c.AD 232

E

Praetorians attempt to capture the eagle of legio ii Parthica, Immae, AD 218

F

Front rankers of legio ii Traiana attack persian cataphracts, battle of Rhesaina, Mesopotamia, AD 243

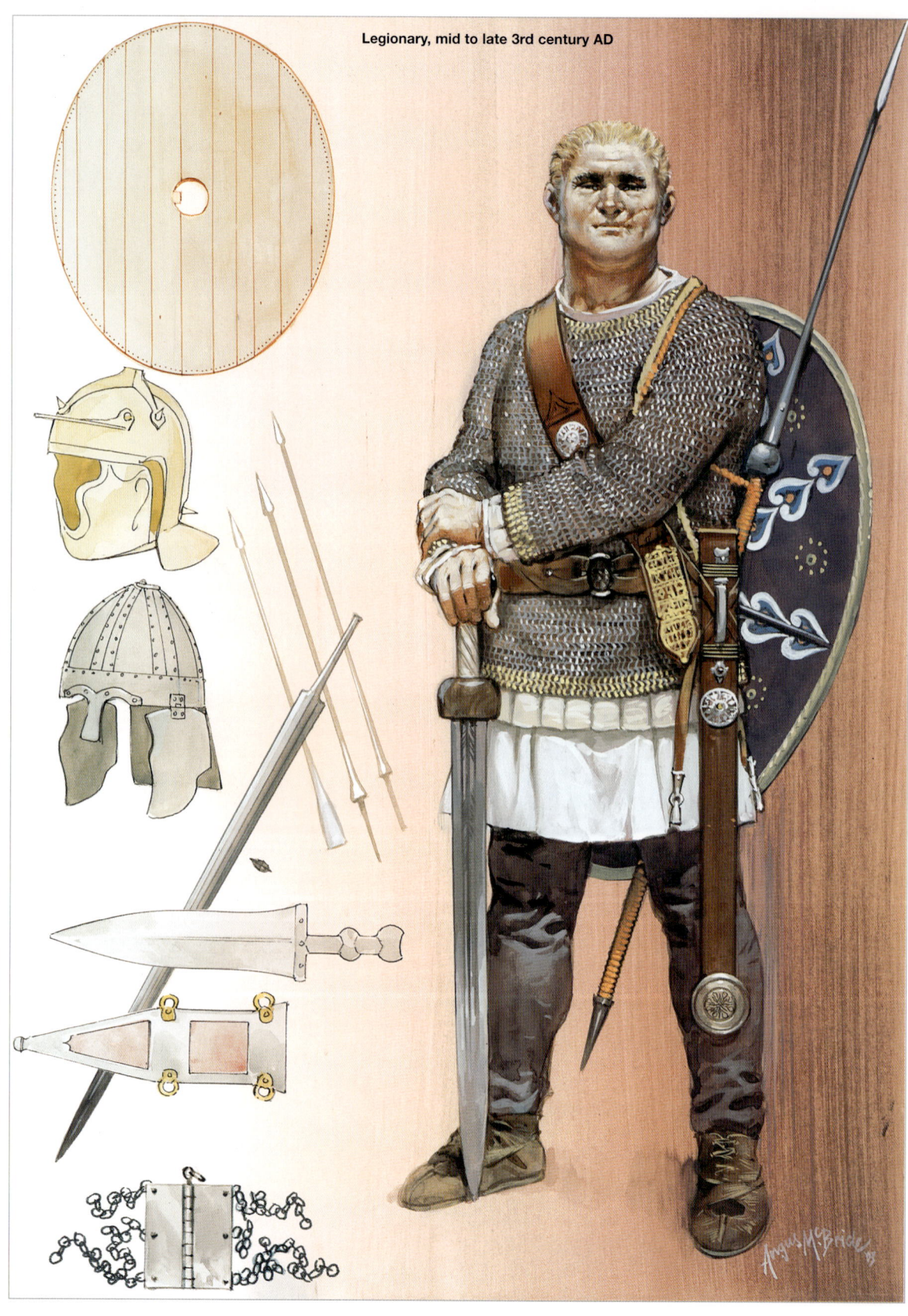

Legionary, mid to late 3rd century AD

H

Like previous generations, the legionaries at Strasbourg only used the sword to slash when pursuing broken troops (ibid., 16.12.52). Ammianus also clarifies another issue. He refers to the medium-length or long sword as the *gladius*, not *spatha*, the term used by modern scholars.

Notably, from the reign of Severus, ordinary soldiers ceased to wear their swords on the right, and wore them on the left, something that was previously the preserve of centurions and senior officers.

A notable continuity in weaponry during our period is the dagger (*pugio*). In the third quarter of the 3rd century it was still modelled after its ancient Spanish prototype (the Romans had adopted the dagger during the Punic Wars of the 3rd century BC). The metal scabbard of the dagger even retained its suspension rings. With blade lengths of up to 30cm (12in) this was a formidable sidearm, and very much part of the military identity (cf. Herodian, 2.13.10).

Helmet and armour

Defensive equipment became more substantial during our period. Ring-mail shirts commonly had full-length sleeves and could extend far down the thighs, while scale cuirasses were reinforced with chest plates. The use of the famous *lorica segmentata*, an articulated armour of iron plates and hoops, was limited but continued until at least the middle of the 3rd century. Supplementary protection for limbs was afforded by articulated arm guards (*manicae*), greaves and even thigh guards.

Helmets also became more substantial. Production of the Imperial Italic series of helmets ceased in the early 3rd century and all legionaries adopted heavier helmets of single bowl construction, reinforced by cross-pieces, and with very deep napes, leaving only a small t-shaped opening for the face (Plates G and H). They offered excellent protection for the head and neck, but the cheek pieces would obscure peripheral vision and their design did not include ear holes. The depth of the nape made it difficult or impossible for the wearer to adopt a crouched fighting position. Such helmets predominated until the closing years of

LEFT **Painted *scutum* from Dura-Europos after restoration. The lion emblem may connect it with legio XVI Flavia but IV Scythica is the last legionary presence attested in the city (254). Deposited 255–57. (Dura-Europos Collection, Yale University Art Gallery)**

Detail from the Portonaccio Battle Sarcophagus, c.180–85. Perhaps commissioned by one of Marcus Aurelius' leading generals but never finished. A legionary centurion in *lorica segmentata* thrusts his sword into a German. Now housed in the Palazzo Massimo, Museo Nazionale Romano, Rome. (Author's collection)

the 3rd century when they were replaced with ridge helmets and *spagenhelmes* (see plate H). These helmets, adopted from the Sassanian Persians and the Sarmatians, were of poor quality in comparison to earlier patterns but their multi-part bowls could simply be riveted together, and neck guards and cheek pieces were attached by leather straps. Such equipment was a response to the financial crisis faced by Diocletian and the need to replace the huge amount of equipment lost in the many disasters of the 3rd century.

Appearance

During the reigns of Marcus Aurelius, Commodus and Septimius Severus (161–211), many legionaries wore full beards and bushy hair after the style of the emperors, but in the reign of Caracalla a new military look emerged of short-cropped hair and light beard. This was the predominant fashion of the 3rd century. Caracalla is also credited by Dio with introducing a new 'uniform' of long-sleeved tunic and the heavy *sagum*

cloak, which fastened at the right shoulder (Dio, 78.3.3). However, the long-sleeved tunic is evident on military gravestones from the mid-2nd century, and the use of the *sagum* probably spread to the infantry from the cavalry. In the 3rd century, tunic long stripes (*clavi*) were replaced with darts at the shoulders and bands of decoration were added to the cuffs and hem. Some designs may have been specific to the military but otherwise the soldier's clothing was little different to that of the civilian.

The colour of military tunics remains unresolved. In the colour plates in this volume ordinary legionaries are conveniently depicted in off-white tunics, centurions and senior officers in red tunics. However, this view has been challenged by G. Sumner, in Men-at-Arms 374: *Roman Military Clothing (1)* (2002), and Men-at-Arms 390: *Roman Military Clothing (2)* (2003), as too simplistic and he has collected much evidence to show a wide range of colours, but one piece of evidence indicates continuity with the past. On the occasion of Gallienus' *decennalia* (celebration of his entering his tenth year in power) in 262 in Rome, his soldiers paraded in white (Historia Augusta, *The Two Gallieni*, 7.1). This recalls how in 69 the victorious legionaries of Vitellius marched into Rome in all their finery, wearing military decorations and led by chief centurions dressed in white (Tacitus, *Histories*, 2.89).

The key to military identification remained the *balteus* or *cingulum* (military belt and baldric; Herodian, 2.13.10). These were decorated with open-work plates, roundels and terminals being attached to long strap-ends (replacing the old apron). During the reign of Severus the ring buckle was introduced and this became the symbol of the soldier until the end of the third century (Plates B, D–H).

BATTLE

Dura-Europos

Sometime between 255 and 257, the Sassanid Persians besieged and captured the Roman fortress city of Dura-Europos. Lying on the River Euphrates Dura was the Romans' most easterly possession in Syria. It was captured from the Parthians in 165 following a great pitched battle (Lucian, *How to Write History*, 15, 19), and the city still bears evidence of repairs made in mud brick after the Romans breached the walls and stormed the city. The city was of great strategic significance because it was positioned on a principal invasion route into Syria and Mesopotamia, and had economic importance as a customs point on the main trade route between East and West.

In the 3rd century an auxiliary cohort, cohors XX Palmyrenorum, garrisoned the city. This unit was over 1,000 strong, contained cavalry and camel riders (dromedaries) but was predominantly infantry. From *c.*208–9 legionary vexillations reinforced the garrison, but it seems that only legio IV Scythica maintained a permanent vexillation at Dura. This numbered at least 300 men. In 233 legionaries of IV Scythica took part in an invasion of Persian territory and were defeated south of Dura, perhaps near to the Persian capital of Ctesiphon. The Sassanid Persians had completely defeated their Parthian overlords in 224–26 and their king Ardashir immediately announced his intention to conquer those Roman territories in Asia and even Europe that had once belonged to the Persian empire destroyed by Alexander the Great. Roman troops stationed in Mesopotamia defected to Ardashir, a charismatic and successful war leader, and he may

Pedestal reliefs from the Arch of Septimius Severus (203) showing Roman soldiers with Parthian prisoners. The soldier to the left wears a *paenula* cloak, *caligae* (heavy military sandals) and a short sword worn on the right – rather antiquated forms of dress and equipment. (Author's collection)

have influenced others to mutiny and kill Flavius Heracleo, the governor of the province in *c*.228 (Dio, 80.3–4). The legions of the province, I and III Parthica, may have received the honorific titles *Severiana Alexandrina* from the emperor for defeating the mutinous troops (Fitz 1983: 139). Ardashir and his son Shapur invaded and occupied Mesopotamia in 229. The Romans counter-attacked in 231. One Roman field army headed by Severus Alexander recaptured Mesopotamia and a second marched through Armenia to invade the Persian territory of Media (northern Iran) where it caused chaos. By 233 a third army was marching south down the Euphrates probably with the objective of capturing the Persian capital, Ctesiphon (20 miles south of modern Baghdad). The Persians concentrated their forces to defend it:

Gold *aureus* of Victorinus celebrating the loyalty of legio XXX Ulpia. The legion's support was crucial in his challenge against Postumus in 268. The coin shows Jupiter armed with a thunderbolt and the legion's Capricorn emblem, (Hunter Coin Cabinet, University of Glasgow)

As there was no sign of … resistance, the Roman army grew somewhat careless on the march, expecting that the third army with [the emperor Severus] Alexander [which was the largest and strongest] had invaded the central lands of the barbarians, and because the enemy were always being diverted to that trouble-spot, it would leave them an easier and safer advance. All the troops had previously been instructed to make a flanking movement into the territory, and a rendezvous had been fixed where they should meet, once the territory between them was also under control. But Alexander failed them by not invading with his army … The Persian king attacked the army with his entire force [of heavily armoured cavalry and horse archers], catching them by surprise and surrounding them in a trap. Under fire from all sides, the Roman soldiers were destroyed because they were unable to stand up to the superior numbers and were continually having to shield with their weapons their exposed [right-hand] sides that formed a target for the enemy. Under the circumstances saving one's skin was preferable to fighting. In the end they were all driven into a mass and fought from behind a wall of shields, as though they were in a siege. Bombarded from every direction and suffering casualties, they held out bravely for as long as they could. But finally they were all destroyed. This terrible disaster, which no one cares to recall, was a set-back to the Romans, since a vast army, matching anything in earlier generations for courage and endurance, had been destroyed. (Herodian, 6.5.5–10, after Whittaker 1969–70)

Herodian's account is deliberately exaggerated to emphasise the failure of Severus Alexander. The battle perhaps ended in stalemate with both sides sustaining major casualties, for the Persians did not follow up their 'victory' and only resumed operations against Rome in 238–39. But we do know that the prefect of legio IV Scythica was killed in the battle for he was commemorated at Dura (Speidel, M.A., 1998, no. 18).

From 239 the garrison of Dura was involved in renewed warfare with the Persians. A graffito from the city records that in that year 'the Persians fell upon us' and Iulius Terentius, the tribune commanding cohors XX Palmyrenorum, was killed in battle. His gravestone commemorates him as 'brave in campaigns and mighty in wars' (*AE* 1948: 124). The Persians do not appear to have captured the city, but they did raid deep into Syria and occupied the major cities of Mesopotamia to the north. Only in 242 did the Romans move against them, having been involved in the civil war from which the teenager Gordian III emerged as a puppet emperor, as well as fighting against the Germans and Goths in Europe. In 243 Shapur was defeated in a major battle at Rhesaina (Ammianus Marcellinus, 23.5.17), and the Romans retook the cities of Mesopotamia by storm. Typically, the Romans invaded Persian territory determined to capture Ctesiphon (244) but Shapur was victorious and recorded his triumph on a great inscription:

> The Caesar Gordian raised from the whole Roman Empire and the nations of the Goths and Germans an army and marched against Assyria, against the nation of the Iranians and against us. A great battle took place between the two sides on the frontiers of Assyria at Meshike [al-Anbar, Iraq]. Caesar Gordian was destroyed and the Roman army annihilated. The Romans proclaimed [the praetorian prefect] Philip [as] Caesar. ('Res Gestae Divi Saporis', 6–9, after Dodgeon & Lieu 1991: 35)

Philip sued for peace and agreed to pay tribute to Shapur. The emperor is depicted in a rock sculpture at Bishapur in Iran kneeling in submission before the mounted Persian king, whilst Gordian lies dead beneath Shapur's warhorse.

The garrison of Dura was temporarily reinforced in 251 by cohors II Ulpia *equitata*, a part-mounted infantry unit, and a vexillation from cohors II Paphlagonum. The records of cohors XX Palmyrenorum suggest that it took casualties at this time (Fink, *RMR* 83) and might even have been reinforced with mercenary Parthian and Armenian cataphracts, heavily armoured cavalry who fought with lance and bow (Speidel, M.P., 1987: 198–201). The Persians were particularly strong in this arm and the Romans with their predominantly infantry forces were always hard pressed to raise suitable numbers of cavalry to counter them (see Plate G).

In 252 Shapur again invaded Roman territory. Following the death of Decius and the destruction of his army by Kniva's Goths at the Abrittus in 251, the new emperor Trebonianus Gallus had to buy peace from the Goths and was unable to pay Shapur his tribute. In 252 Shapur consequently invaded Roman territory again and defeated a massive Roman field army mustering at Barbalissos and proceeded to capture the eastern capital of Antioch near to the Mediterranean coast. Zeugma, where legio IV Scythica had its base, was destroyed but whether much of the legion was there at the time is uncertain; some vexillations would have been at Barbalissos, while others garrisoned towns and cities across Syria.

The latest dated document from Dura shows that a vexillation of IV Scythica was in the city in 254. The document actually records the divorce of Iulius Antiochus, a soldier of the legion, from the local woman Aurelia Amimma on 30 April 254. One of the witnesses to the document was a soldier named Patroclianus, perhaps another legionary (*P. Dura*, 32). That legionaries were marrying local women shows they were based in the city for considerable periods of time, perhaps permanently, and Antiochus and Patroclianus may have still been present when the Persians attacked for the last time between 255 and 257. The following reconstruction of the siege derives entirely from the archaeological evidence amassed during the Franco-American excavations of the city in the 1930s (Rostovtzeff et al. 1936: 188–205; Coulston 2001).

Skirmishing took place between the Romans and Persians outside the city – scale horse-armour was discovered with an arrowhead lodged in it – but the Persians were evidently too strong in number and the Romans retreated to their fortifications.

The Persians appear to have attacked Tower 19 first. They dug a siege mine beginning some 40m from the tower. The flat terrain of the desert made the spoil from the mine clearly visible to the Romans and within easy range of missiles, but the spoil heap protected the mouth of the mine. The Persians tunnelled until they reached the foot of the tower then dug galleries under the north-west corner of it and under 15m of the city wall. Shored up by wooden posts and planks the Persians intended to fire the mine and cause the tower and wall to collapse, fall forward into the desert and make a massive breach for the Persians to storm into the city. The Romans, alerted by the growing spoil heap, and the increasingly audible scrapings of the Persian sappers as they excavated under the foundations of the tower and wall, dug a counter-mine and determined to seize the Persian mine before it was fired.

The Roman mine met the Persian excavations just under the city wall. Fighting in a tunnel approximately 1.6m wide and high, the soldiers presumably fought at most two or three abreast, only the opposing front ranks being able to fight hand to hand. If they had any light it was from smoky oil lamps or torches. The Romans fought in ring-mail armour, some with additional limb protection, and with shields. None wore helmets; the soldiers had to fight bent forward and the long neck guards of current helmets would have made it impossible to throw back their heads. The Romans carried swords and javelins – presumably used as thrusting weapons – while arrowheads indicate the use of bows. The Persians were similarly equipped but also wore helmets, for these had flexible mail at the neck rather than plate metal (James 1986).

What happened in the tunnel is not entirely clear but it seems that the Roman counter-mine broke through and a fight ensued in which the Romans were defeated, leaving 16–18 dead or wounded behind. In the dark and claustrophobic tunnel it would not be surprising if some of the Romans simply panicked, turned and attempted to flee, turning their column into a confused mass and making them easy victims for the Persians. In order to prevent the Persians from using the counter-mine to enter the city the Romans hastily blocked up the entrance. Inside the counter-mine, the Persians stacked the Roman casualties near to the blocked entrance, creating a barrier if the

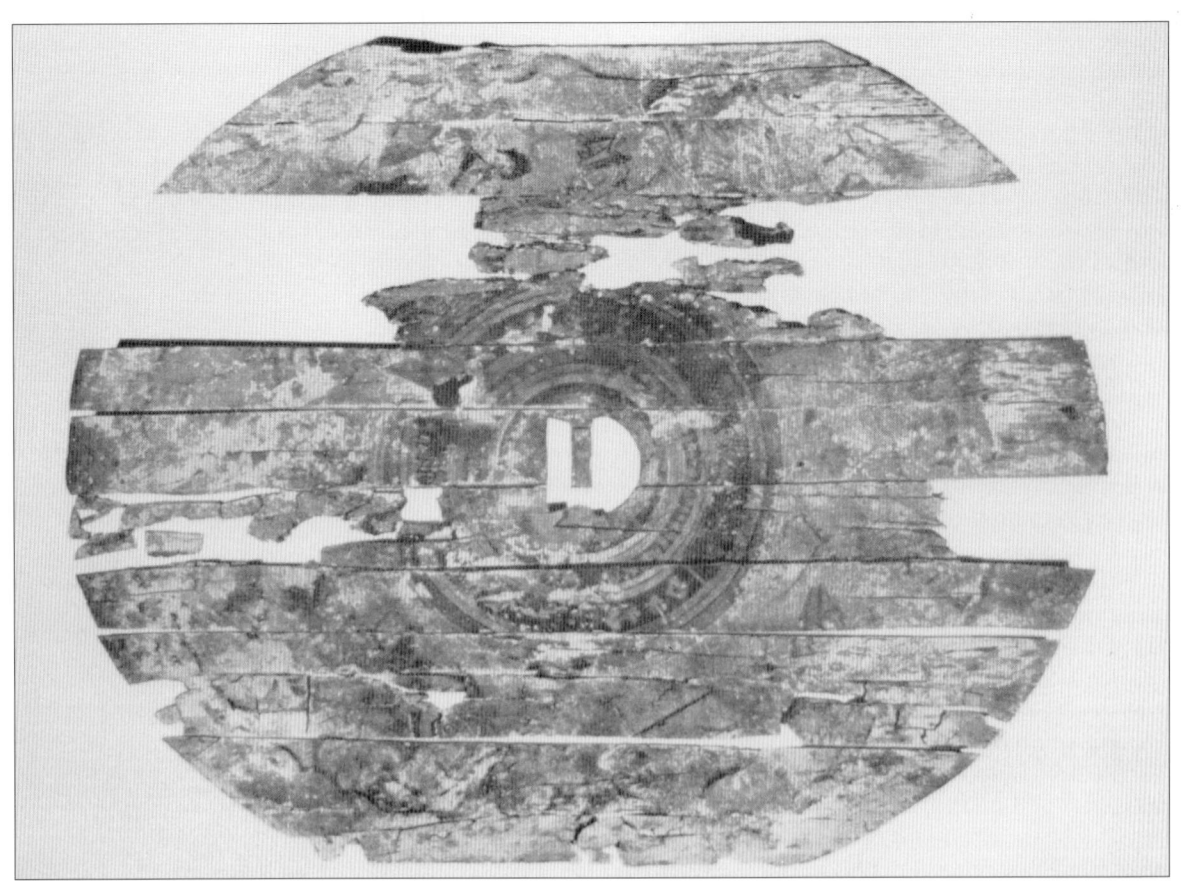

Oval shield of plank construction
from Dura-Europos, 255–57.
(Dura-Europos Collection, Yale
University Art Gallery)

Romans decided to attempt another attack and to clear the way for
firing the wooden supports; to do so they used a pile of Roman cloaks
and sulphur (*pers. comm.* Simon James). The counter-mine was partially
destroyed by the fire, and the Persians blocked the still open section
nearest to their mine with stone blocks prised from the foundations of
the tower and city wall.

Strangely, the Persians appear to have left one of their own dead
behind in the counter-mine. His skeleton was discovered fallen on its
back away from the city as if he had been killed facing it, indicating that
he was an attacker. His long mail coat was pulled up around his chest as
if a comrade had attempted to drag him back towards the Persian mine,
but perhaps the fire had been set and fearing asphyxiation the soldier
attempting to drag the body clear was forced to abandon it.

The Persians were thus free to fire their mine. Perhaps because of
lack of ventilation the fire did not burn throughout the mine with
equal intensity, for sections survived intact, but the tower and wall did
collapse. Yet this success was only partial because in anticipation of the
siege the Romans had reinforced the city wall on both sides with
massive earthen and mud-brick ramparts. The rampart inside the wall
actually engulfed all the buildings built against it. The ramparts
prevented the tower and section of undermined wall from falling into
the desert and forming a massive breach. Instead the wall sank 1m into
the ground, and the north-west corner of the tower collapsed 2.5m
into the gallery dug below it. This at least denied its use to the Romans

as an artillery platform. Numerous catapult bolts, stone balls, arrowheads and shafts survive from the site indicating the intense volume of fire maintained by both sides.

The Persians then proceeded to completely undermine Tower 14 at the southern end of the desert wall, and by bringing it down protected their right flank (i.e. the unshielded side) from archery as they built a massive ramp of soil and debris dug from the cemetery outside the city. The ramp rose above the crenellations of the wall but the Romans built a wall of mud-brick to counter it. They also attempted to undermine the ramp, but their two mines appear to have been intercepted by the Persians, who may finally have entered the city through the Roman excavations. Exhausted by a siege lasting several months, the garrison probably surrendered for there is little evidence of destruction in the city to suggest that the Persians took it by storm. It is probable that the surviving garrison and the civilian population were deported to Persia, which was the fate of the emperor Valerian's field army in 260 when it was defeated outside Edessa. There is much evidence for major construction work carried out by Roman prisoners of war in the Sassanian Empire, ranging from the building of great dams and bridges to the construction of new cities. Even Shapur's famous victory reliefs at Bishapur, displaying the defeated emperors Gordian, Philip and Valerian, and Roman prisoners, are thought to exhibit Roman workmanship (Ball 2000: 115–23).

Dura-Europos was abandoned. The Persians made no attempt to occupy it after 257 and the Romans never reclaimed it. The city was too exposed and the continual warfare had diverted trade elsewhere. The region around the city became a kind of no-man's land. Ammianus passed Dura in 363 when marching on Ctesiphon with the emperor Julian but described it only as a deserted city (Ammianus Marcellinus, 23.7.8).

Legion versus cavalry

In 260 Shapur defeated and captured the emperor Valerian at Edessa, then captured Antioch for a second time. His army divided into raiding columns that plundered their way across Syria and the provinces of what is now Turkey. Only when they were returning home did the Romans manage to rally under Macrianus and Ballista, and a number of the plunder-laden columns were defeated. Odaenathus, king of Palmyra, made the only real successes against the Persians. Palmyra was a rich semi-independent city within Syria. Its wealth stemmed from its location at an oasis in the desert making it a key hub for all the major trade routes and the rulers of the city grew rich on the trade that passed through their city. The Palmyrenes also organised trade caravans and policed the routes with mounted

Altar from Old Kilpatrick fort on the Antonine Wall. The inscription suggests that Iulius Candidus, centurion of legio I Italica, commanded a detachment of cohors I Baetasiorum, perhaps during the British campaigns of Severus (208–11). I Italica was normally based in Bulgaria. (Hunterian Museum, University of Glasgow)

archers. This continued under Roman rule and it was with his considerable number of Palmyrene troops (archers and cataphracts) and remnants of the Roman forces that Odaenathus pursued Shapur and raided Persian territory between 260 and 267. He may even have besieged Shapur in Ctesiphon. The emperor Gallienus, based in Italy and sandwiched between the breakaway Gallic Empire (from 259) in the west and German and Gothic invaders to the north and east, was forced to cede effective control of his eastern provinces to the Palmyrene king. When Odaenathus was murdered in 267 his wife Zenobia took control and began to consolidate Palmyrene control. By 270 she controlled Arabia and Egypt as well as Syria and was promoting her son Vaballathus as a co-emperor to the legitimate Roman emperor Aurelian. However, the victories of Gallienus, Claudius II and Aurelian over the Germans and Goths in 268–71 briefly secured the central European provinces of the Empire and finally Aurelian marched east to crush Palmyra. The deciding battle was fought at Emesa (272):

> The Palmyrene army was 70,000 strong … [and] mustered in the plain before Emesa. [Aurelian] formed up opposite them with his Dalmatian cavalry, and the [legions of] Moesians and Pannonians … and Noricans and Raetians, which are Celtic legions. In addition … were the praetorians, selected according to merit out of the entire body, the most distinguished of all. Along with these were formed up the Mauretanian cavalry and, from Asia, troops out of Tyana, Mesopotamia, Syria, Phoenicia and Palestine. In addition to their other equipment, the troops from Palestine, had with them clubs and cudgels.
>
> When the armies engaged, the Roman cavalry appeared to retreat so that the Roman army might not fall into a trap and be encircled by the Palmyrene cavalry, who were greatly superior in numbers. The Palmyrene cavalry therefore pursued those who were retreating, and consequently disrupted their own order, but things turned out the opposite to what the Roman cavalry had planned. They were being pursued by an enemy who was far superior to them, and since many were killed, the result was that all the fighting fell to the infantry. Seeing that the line of Palmyrene cavalry was disordered as it committed itself to the pursuit, they wheeled their ranks around and attacked the enemy as it was scattered and confused. There followed a great slaughter as they came on with the customary weapons, except in the case of the Palestinians who wielded their clubs against those in iron and bronze armour [i.e. the cataphracts]. This as much as anything was responsible for the victory, for the enemy was not familiar with the cudgels and were terrified by their impact. The Palmyrenes broke and fled, trampling their own men, as well as being slain by the Romans, so that the plain was filled with the corpses of men and horses. (*Zosimus*, 1.52–53, adapted from Buchanan & Davis 1967)

Emesa demonstrates the continuing quality of Roman infantry. Even with their cavalry in flight, and therefore the protection to their flanks

lost, the legionary and praetorian infantry did not succumb to panic. Aurelian seized the opportunity raised by the Palmyrenes' disorder because he knew his infantry had the discipline to follow the commands relayed by the trumpets and standards, the skill to wheel together without losing the cohesion of the battle line, and the ferocity to win the battle once they charged. That 'they came on with the customary weapons' evokes an image of Roman warfare that had not changed for centuries: the *pila* volley followed by the charge with drawn swords (*RL*, 46–56). In defeating Palmyra Aurelian not only restored the eastern provinces of the Empire but also restored the prestige of Roman arms in the East. He proved that a Roman army, composed mostly of traditional legionary elements, could defeat the seemingly invincible horsemen of the East. It was this victory that propelled Aurelian to the capture of Zenobia and the defeat of Tetricus, the last Gallic emperor at Châlons in 274. Having reunified the Empire, Aurelian was proclaimed 'restorer of the world'.

Antoninianus of Aurelian (270–75) proclaiming the 'harmony of the legions', a sure sign of reconciliation after civil war. The goddess Concordia (Unity) holds two centurial standards. (Hunter Coin Cabinet, University of Glasgow)

AFTERMATH

Emesa illustrates that most casualties in ancient battles were inflicted during the pursuit. When the enemy had broken and run, forsaking his order, abandoning his heavy equipment and trying to escape to anywhere but the battlefield, he was easy prey to the determined pursuer, especially one elated with successful combat. Cavalry were deadly at this stage of the battle.

Having routed Septimius Severus' infantry at Lugdunum in 197, Clodius Albinus' British legionaries 'followed up in pursuit and had begun to chant their hymn of victory, assuming they had already won' (Herodian, 3.7.3). However, the British soldiers, now in disorder themselves, were attacked from the rear by Severus' entire cavalry force which had been detached before the start of the battle to ride around the flank of Albinus' force and attack it in the rear. The British were utterly defeated. Still, the picture of the seemingly victorious legionaries of II Augusta, VI Victrix and XX Valeria Victrix, charging after their fleeing opponents and chanting their song of victory, must stand as one of the most vivid images of the legionary in battle.

However, battles were rarely decisive affairs with one side emerging as the clear-cut victor. Sometimes battles simply fizzled out with neither side able to win an advantage, length of combat being limited by the stamina of the troops involved and the casualties they were prepared to take. During lulls in the fighting temporary treaties could be made to collect the wounded and dead from the ground between the opposing armies (Herodian, 4.15.5–7).

The wounded were treated to a high standard by *medici* (doctors and orderlies). They carried many of the surgical tools familiar to the modern combat surgeon and were capable of performing complex operations, but without the same understanding of hygiene and lacking anaesthetics and powerful antibiotics, the legionary's chances of surviving a major trauma wound were slim (Salazar 2000). Other legionaries were traumatised by the experience of battle:

> Marcus to Antonia, Sarapion, and Cassianos, my parents, many greetings. I make obeisance for you in the presence of the gods sharing the temple. For no one can go up by river to make obeisance, because of the battle which has taken place between the Anoteritae and the soldiers. Fifteen soldiers of the singulares [guardsmen] have died, apart from the legionaries, evocati [reservists], the wounded, and those suffering from battle fatigue.
> (P. Ross. – Georg., III, 1, 1–7, after Davies 1969: 94)

Marcus was a doctor attached to the military and based in Alexandria during the 3rd century. The Anoteritae are otherwise unknown but Marcus' letter provides an excellent snapshot of one of the endemic small wars and rebellions that our major literary sources fail to record. Most interesting is the reference to soldiers suffering 'battle fatigue'. Combat stress is not normally associated with the legionary, whose reputation is such that modern media invariably portray him as the ultimate soldier, remorseless and invincible. But such an image forgets that legionaries were ordinary men, many still in their teens, who having been hastily levied and trained were thrown into a situation of ultimate stress. In the terrifying physical collision of ancient battle, they fought hand to hand, hacked and stabbed, wrestled and bit (cf. Dio, 71.7.4–5). Combatants were always at risk of being trampled or asphyxiated in the crush, accidentally killed by the weapons of their own side and endured a continual hail of arrows, javelins and sling bullets. Soldiers heard the screams of their comrades and watched them die in the most brutal fashion. It is no wonder that some survivors emerged 'shell-shocked' from this experience of supreme mental and physical trauma.

Denarius issued by Clodius Albinus, showing clasped hands holding an aquila, AD 196. The legend celebrates his 'faithful [British] legions'. (Hunter Coin Cabinet, University of Glasgow)

Ordinary legionaries were buried in mass graves at the battle site, though some might be buried in single graves by their *commilitones* (fellow-soldiers), or on the orders of the general if they had shown particular valour in the battle. Centurions and officers received single graves (Appian, *Civil Wars*, 2.82). One such soldier's grave was discovered at Lyon in France. Unusually, the soldier was buried with his sword and other military equipment and coins discovered in the grave dating to 194 suggest he died fighting at Lugdunum in 197 (Wuilleumier 1950).

ABOVE LEFT **Copper *as* of Gordian III celebrating eternal peace and showing Victory standing over the river gods Tigris and Euphrates, referring to the recovery of Mesopotamia from the Persians in 243. (Hunter Coin Cabinet, University of Glasgow)**

ABOVE RIGHT ***Antoninianus* of the British usurper Carausius, showing that he had a vexillation of the German legion I Minervia in his field army in 286. The legion's ram emblem is depicted. (Hunter Coin Cabinet, University of Glasgow)**

It was a disgrace to leave the Roman dead to rot on the field but this did occur when Roman forces were routed. At Gelduba (Krefeld-Gellep in Germany) in *c*.259–60 the cavalry of the garrison fought the Alamanni or Franks to the death on the ground before their fort. They lost and lay beside the carcasses of their horses until Roman forces re-secured the area, dug pits, dragged the half-rotten dead in to them and covered them with lime (Reichmann 1999).

Legionaries normally left instructions in their wills for the erection of funerary monuments and some soldiers may even have posed for full-length portraits prior to going to war. These monuments were usually set up outside base, though the deceased were buried far away. It is these monuments that often tell us most about the ordinary legionary, for in the terse inscriptions and grim portraits we glimpse the character of men who otherwise remain silent, except through the writings of their commanders or historians. These monuments speak of their arrogance, their toughness, their love for family and comrades, but above all their pride in being legionaries.

Legio II Parthica after AD 268

Legio II Parthica was still based at Albanum during the reign of Aurelian (270–75), indicating its continuing relationship with the praetorians in nearby Rome: service in II Parthica still facilitated transfer to the praetorians, (*IGBulg* III, 2, 1570). Aurelian also granted the legion the rare honorific title *Aureliana* (*AE* 1975: 171), showing the esteem in which he held the legion and that it had been crucial to his hold on power during the hard fighting in Italy in 270. A substantial vexillation from the legion should be numbered among the units making up Aurelian's *comitatus* (below). The legion remained close to the emperors in the final years of the 3rd century. It supplied a vexillation to the *comitatus* of Diocletian's co-emperor Maximianus, but along with a praetorian cohort, it defected to the British usurper Carausius in 286. It is most unlikely that this detachment survived to be reunited with its parent formation (Casey 1994: 92ff).

Legio II Parthica was increasingly superseded by Diocletian's new elite legions of Ioviani and Herculiani, and probably supplied drafts of troops to the new formations (note Aurelius Victor, *De Caesaribus*, 39.47). It was the fate of the remainder of legio II Parthica to be transferred to Mesopotamia and downgraded to the status of a frontier unit. This may have already occurred when Constantine defeated Maxentius at the battle of the Milvian Bridge outside Rome in 312, but following his victory he disbanded the praetorians for good. It is tempting to see the transfer of II Parthica to the East as a punishment for fighting against him. Constantine later donated the deserted barracks of II Parthica and the empty houses of the soldiers' families at Albanum to the Church (*Liber Pontificalis*, 34.30).

In Mesopotamia the already reduced legion was broken up into 'micro-legions' and slowly eroded away in the endless Persian wars. One such micro-legion, perhaps of 500–1,000 men, stubbornly defended the town of Bezabde in Mesopotamia from Shapur II in 360, but the city was stormed and the surviving legionaries were deported to Persia (Ammianus Marcellinus, 20.7). The fate of the last remnant of II Parthica, stationed at a place called Cepha, is unknown (Notitia Dignitatum, *Oriens*, 36.30).

Antoninianus of Aurelian (270–75) proclaiming the 'harmony of the legions'. The goddess Concordia (Unity) holds four centurial standards. (Hunter Coin Cabinet, University of Glasgow)

The demise of legio II Parthica in Mesopotamia was inevitable, but for almost a century it was virtually the personal legion of the emperors and honoured as such. Let us finish here with Dexippus' description of Aurelian's 'chosen army' (*comitatus*) in which legio II Parthica, the *lanciarii* and many other legionary vexillations played such a crucial role:

> When the Roman emperor Aurelian heard about the advent of the embassy from the Iuthungi, he said that he would deliberate about them until the next day; he then arrayed his soldiers as if for war, so that he might alarm the enemy. When the arrangement satisfied him, he ascended a high dais, raised far above the ground, and, donning his purple robe, arranged all the troops around him. All those who held some command stood beside him, all on their horses. Behind the emperor were the standards of the chosen army. These were golden eagles and imperial images and the army registers inscribed in gold letters; all of these things were displayed on silver shafts. And when everything was arranged in this way, he requested that the Iuthungi should come forward. It so happened that when they saw this they were amazed and stayed silent for a long time. (Dexippus, *FGrH* II.2, no. 100, fr. 6, translated by Kathleen McLaughlin)

WEBSITES

The most extensive collection of relevant finds in the UK is to be found in the British Museum in London: http://www.thebritishmuseum.ac.uk

The Hunterian Museum at the University of Glasgow has considerable numismatic material relating to our period, and an important collection of Roman military equipment from the Antonine Wall: http://www.hunterian.gla.ac.uk

The Croy Hill relief (see Plate A) and a major collection of Roman material from the Antonine period to the early 3rd century can be found at the Museum of Scotland in Edinburgh: http://www.nms.ac.uk

Armamentarium, run under the auspices of the University of Newcastle, is a site dedicated to Roman arms and armour and contains the best guide to museums across Europe with relevant material: http://museums.ncl.ac.uk/archive/armamentarium

Those wishing to find out more about re-enactors, displays and the reconstruction of equipment are advised to visit the site of Arbeia Roman Fort and Museum at South Shields, home of third century re-enactment group cohors V Gallorum: http://www.twmuseums.org.uk/arbeia/index.html

For further information on Dura-Europos and discussion of the Roman Army visit Simon James' excellent home page: http://www.le.ac.uk/ar/stj/index.html

The most useful on-line bibliography of the armies of Greece and Rome is Hugh Elton's Warfare in the Ancient World: http://www.fiu.edu/~eltonh/army.html

Gary Brueggeman's website is excellent for those wishing to investigate Roman tactics and fighting styles: http://www.geocities.com/Athens/Oracle/6622/

GLOSSARY

aquila eagle standard of the legion.

aquilifer eagle-bearer.

balteus military belt (sometimes called a *cingulum*), identifies a man as a soldier.

beneficiarius soldier in receipt of *beneficium* (favour) of an officer. Could act as a clerk in the legions, though there were numerous specialist duties.

canabae civil settlement outside a fort.

century (centuria) sub-unit of the legion comprising 80 soldiers, 59 per legion.

centurion (centurio) commander of the century.

cohort (cohors) formation of 6 centuries/3 maniples, 10 per legion.

comitatus The field army attached to the emperor's court. For much of our period built around the praetorians and legio II Parthica with vexillations detached from the legions and auxiliary units.

commilito fellow-soldier; expression of comradeship, applied across the board from ordinary soldiers to generals and the emperor.

contubernium sub-unit of the century comprised of eight men who shared a room/tent.

dilectus levy, conscription.

dolabra military pickaxe.

duplicarius soldier receiving double pay, e.g. *optio*, *signifer*.

Equestrian Order later Republican and Imperial Rome's 'middle' or business class, originally signifying men whose wealth was sufficient to equip themselves as cavalrymen. Equestrians were superior in class to ordinary soldiers (*caligati*); hence they could be promoted directly to *centurionates* (and higher ranks) without prior experience.

expediti lightly equipped soldiers.

gladius general term for a sword.

hasta spear.

hastatus 'spear-armed', centurial title.

lanciarius, legionary equipped with a light javelin (*lancea*).

legate (legatus) senatorial commander of the legion.

legio legion, chief formation of the Roman Army, comprised of 59 centuries organised in 10 cohorts, the first of approximately double strength. Optimum manpower was 5,240 (including 120 cavalry) but probably rarely achieved.

lorica armour: *hamata* – mail; *squamata* – scale; '*segmentata*' – articulated.

medici generic term for medical staff including high-ranking doctors and junior orderlies.

optio centurion's deputy, one per century.

pilum legionary javelin.

pilus 'spear/javelin-armed', centurial title.

posterior 'rear', centurial title.

praefectus equestrian commander of a legion.

praemia discharge bonus/pension.

primi ordines front/first rankers, centurions of first cohort.

primus pilus 'first spear or *pilum*', leading centurion of the first cohort and most senior in the legion. Tax official from c.280.

princeps 'foremost', centurial title.

principales under and junior officers including the *tesserarius*, *optio* and *signifer*.

prior 'front', centurial title.

pugio dagger.

sagittarius archer.

sagum military cloak.

scutum curved legionary shield.

Senatorial Order/Senate ruling class and council of Rome, comprised of annually elected magistrates, chiefly consuls, praetors, aediles and tribunes, and ex-magistrates, who respectively directed or advised on Roman policy. Senators were superseded by self-made equestrians (i.e. men promoted to the order via military service) in the later 3rd century.

sesquiplicarius soldier receiving pay and a half, e.g. *tesserarius*.

signifer standard-bearer, one per century.

signum standard.

spatha medium-length or long sword.

tesserarius officer of the watchword, one per century.

tiro recruit.

tribune (tribunus) legionary officer; 6 per legion

vexillatio – vexillation, detachment from a legion or cohort.

vexillum flag standard of a detachment.

vitis the vine wood staff of the centurion, indicative of his rank.

BIBLIOGRAPHY

AE = *L'Année Épigraphique.*

Alston, R.A., 1994: 'Roman military pay from Caesar to Diocletian', *Journal of Roman Studies* 84, 113–23.

Ball, W., 2000: *Rome in the East: The Transformation of an Empire* (London).

Balty, J.C., 1988: 'Apamea in Syria in the Second and Third Centuries AD', *JRS* 78, 91–104.

Balty, J.C., & Van Rengen, R., 1993: *Apamea in Syria, the Winter quarters of Legio II Parthica. Roman Gravestones from the Military Cemetery* (Brussels).

Bennett, P.A., et al., 1982: *Excavations at Canterbury Castle*, vol. 1 (Maidstone).

Bishop, M.C., & Coulston, J.N.C., 1993: *Roman Military Equipment from the Punic Wars to the Fall of Rome* (London).

Brunt, P.A., 1974: 'Conscription and Volunteering in the Roman Imperial Army', *Scripta Classica Israelica* 1, 90–115, in Brunt 1990: *Roman Imperial Themes*, 188–214, with addenda on 512–15.

Bruun, C., 1995: '*Pericula Alexandrina*: The Adventures of a Recently Discovered Centurion of *Legio II Parthica*', *Arctos* 29, 9–27.

Buchanan, J.J., & Davies, H.T., 1967: *Zosimus: Historia Nova* (San Antonio).

Casey, J., 1994: *Carausius and Allectus: The British Usurpers* (London).

CIL = *Corpus Inscriptionum Latinarum.*

Cooper, P., 1968: *The Origins of the 'New' Roman Army in the Third Century* (D.Phil. thesis, Oxford University).

Coulston, J.C.N., 1985: 'Roman Archery Equipment' in M. Bishop (ed.) 1985: 'The Production and Distribution of Roman Military Equipment' (*BAR* S275), 280–325.

Coulston, J.C.N., 1995: 'The sculpture of an armoured figure at Alba Iulia, Romania', *Arma* 7, 13–17.

Coulston, J.C.N., 2001: 'The Archaeology of Roman Conflict' in P. Freeman & A. Pollard (eds.) 2001: *Fields of Conflict: Progress and Prospect in Battlefield Archaeology*, BAR Int. Ser. 958 (Oxford), 23–50.

Cowan, R.H., 2002: *Aspects of the Severan Field Army* (Ph.D. thesis, University of Glasgow).

Cowan, R.H, 2003: *Roman Legionary, 58 BC–AD 69* (Oxford, 2003)

Davies, R.W., 1969: 'The Medici of the Roman Armed Forces', *Epigraphische Studien* 8, 83–99.

Dodgeon, M.H., & Lieu, S.N.C., 1991: *The Roman Eastern Frontier and the Persian Wars, AD 226–363. A Documentary History* (London)

Engelhardt, C., 1865: *Nydam Mosefund* (Copenhagen).

Engelhardt, C., 1869: *Vimose Fundet* (Copenhagen).

Fink, RMR = Fink, R.O., 1971: *The Roman Military Records on Papyrus* (Cleveland).

FGrH = Jacoby, F. (ed.), *Die Fragmente der Griechischen Historiker* (Berlin & Leiden, 1923 to present).

Fitz, J., 1983: *Honorific Titles of Roman Military Units in the Third Century* (Budapest and Bonn)

Horbacz, T.J., & Oledzki, M., 1998: 'Roman Inlaid Swords', *Journal of Roman Military Equipment Studies* 9, 19–30.

IGBulg = Mihailov, G. (ed.), *Inscriptiones Graececae in Bulgaria Repertae* (Sofia, 1956–70).

Ilkjær, J., 1989: 'The Weapons Sacrifice from Illerup Ådal, Denmark', in K. Randsborg (ed.), 1989: *The Birth of Europe* (Rome), 54–61.

ILS = Dessau, H. (ed.), *Inscriptiones Latinae Selectae* (Berlin, 1892–1916).

James, S., 1986: 'Evidence from Dura-Europos for the Origins of Late Roman Helmets', Syria 63, 107–34.

James, S., 1987: 'Dura-Europos and the Introduction of the Mongolian Release' in M. Dawson (ed.) 1987: *Roman Military Equipment: The Accoutrements of War* (*BAR* Int. Ser. 336), 77–83.

Kennedy, D.L., 1987: 'The garrisoning of Mesopotamia in the late Antonine and early Severan period', *Antichthon* 21, 57–66.

Keppie, L.J.F., 1997: 'The changing face of the Roman legions', *Papers of the British School at Rome* 65, 89–102 = Keppie 2000: *Legions and Veterans: Roman Army Papers 1971–2000*, Mavors 12 (Stuttgart), 50–63.

Mann, J.C., 1963: 'The Raising of New Legions During the Principate', Hermes 91, 175–83 = Mann, J.C., 1996: *Britain and the Roman Empire* (Aldershot).

Mann, J.C., 1999: 'A Note on the Legion IV Italica', *Zeitschrift für Papyrologie* 126, 228.

Mócsy, A., 1974: *Pannonia and Upper Moesia* (London).

Okamura, L., 1996: 'Roman Withdrawals From Three Transfluvial Frontiers', in R. Mathisen & S. Hagith (eds.), 1996: *Shifting Frontiers in Late Antiquity* (Aldershot), 11–19.

P. Beatty Panop. = Skeat, T.C. (ed.), 1964: *Papyri from Panopolis in the Chester Beatty Library, Dublin* (Dublin).

P. Dura = C.B. Welles et al.: *The Excavations at Dura Europos. Final Report V, Part 1: The Parchments and Papyri* (New Haven, 1959).

P. Ross. Georg = Papyri russischer und georgischer Sammlungen (Tiflis, 1925–35)

Pollard, N., 2000: *Soldier and Civilian in Roman Syria* (Ann Arbor).

Reichmann, C., 1999: 'Archäologische Spuren der sogenennanten Bataverschlacht vom November 69 n. Chr. und von Kämpfen des 3. Jahrhunderts n. Chr. im Umfeld Kastells *Gelduba* (Krefeld-Gellep)' in W. Schlüter & R. Wiegels (eds.), 1999: *Rom, Germanien und die Ausgrabungen von Kalkriese* (Osnabrück), 97–115.

Robinson, H.R., 1975: *The Armour of Imperial Rome* (London).

Rostovtzeff, M.I., et al., 1936: *The Excavations at Dura-Europos, Preliminary Report of the Sixth Season of Work, October 1931–March 1932* (New Haven).

Salazer, C.F., 2000: *The Treatment of War Wounds in Graeco-Roman Antiquity* (Leiden).

Šašel, J., 1961: *'Bellum Serdicense'*, Situla 4, 3–30.

Saxer, R., 1967: *Untersuchungen zu den Vexillationen des römischen Kaiserheeres von Augustus bis Diokletian*, Epigraphische Studien 1 (Köln).

Speidel, M.A., 1992: 'Roman Army Pay Scales', *Journal of Roman Studies* 82, 87–106.

Speidel, M.A., 1998: 'Legio IIII Scythica, its movements and men' in D. Kennedy et al.: *The Twin Towns of Zeugma on the Euphrates* (Journal of Roman Archaeology Supplementary Series no. 27), 163–204.

Speidel, M.P., 1987: 'The Rise of the Mercenaries in the Third Century', *Tyche* 2, 191–201 = Speidel, M.P., 1992: 71–81.

Speidel, M.P., 1990: 'The Army at Aquileia, the Moesiaci Legion, and the Shield Emblems in the Notitia Dignitatum', *Saalburg-Jahrbuch* 45, 68–72 = Speidel, M.P., 1992: 414–18.

Speidel, M.P., 1992: *Roman Army Studies II*, Mavors 8 (Stuttgart).

Speidel, M.P., 1992a: *The Framework of an Imperial Legion* (Caerleon).

Stephenson, I.P., 1999: *Roman Infantry Equipment: The Later Empire* (Stroud).

Sumner, G., 2002–3: *Roman Military Clothing*, 2 volumes (Oxford).

Ulbert, G., 1974: 'Straubing und Nydam. Zu römischen Langschwerten der späten Limeszeit', in Kossack, G, & Ulbert, G. (eds.), 1974: *Studien zur Vor- und Frühgeschichtlichen Archäologie. Festschrift für Joachim Werner zum 65. Geburtstag* (München), 197–216.

Whittaker, C.R., 1969–70: *Herodian: Roman History* (Loeb Classical Library, London).

Wuilleumier, M.P., 1950: 'Lyon: La bataille de 197', *Gallia* 8, 146–8.

COLOUR PLATE COMMENTARY

A: LEGIONARIES MID-2ND CENTURY AD

This plate is based on a relief of three legionaries carved on a sandstone slab from Croy Hill on the Antonine Wall in Scotland.

All three legionaries carry heavy flat-tanged *pila* and their cylindrical shields (*scuta*) are decorated with rosettes and Capricorn emblems derived from distance slabs set up on the Antonine Wall by legio II Augusta to commemorate completed sectors of rampart, *c.*142. The men wear heavy hooded *paenula* cloaks, secured by buttons at the chest. Their *caligae* sandals are represented on victory monuments of the later 2nd century but this traditional legionary footwear might actually have gone out of use in the years before the Antonine Wall was built.

The central legionary is a centurion, identified by his red tunic and because he wears his old-style Pompeii *gladius* on the left. This sword was now going out of service. His short ring-mail shirt is supplemented with pteruges to protect the upper arms and abdomen. His belt has enamelled plates based on the finds from Newstead in Scotland (see detail) and the large dagger anticipates the 3rd century form (after the handle from Bar Hill on the Antonine Wall). The helmet slung over his shield is an Imperial Gallic G, perhaps 75 years old, but such heavy items of equipment could remain in service for considerable periods.

The legionary to the left wears a padded garment (*thoracomachus* or *subarmilis*), probably of linen stuffed with wool, and normally worn under mail or other armour, but was probably considered adequate protection when manoeuvrability was necessary. His ring-pommel short sword is carried in a scabbard with a peltate-shaped chape and suspended by a dolphin-shaped scabbard slide. The slide and ring-pommel swords were probably adopted from the Sarmatians and other trans-Danubian opponents. The details illustrate short and heavy forms of the swords and the intricate engraved or inlaid decoration they might receive. His belt is decorated with open-work plates from Newstead and his helmet follows the example from Theilenhofen in Germany, illustrating the transition from the Imperial-type helmet to the 'cavalry' type (see detail).

The legionary to the right is protected by a cuirass of *lorica segmentata* of Newstead pattern, a simpler and more robust development of the Corbridge patterns used in the previous century. His helmet is an iron Imperial Italic G, based on the example from Hebron and probably lost during the Bar Kokhba revolt of 132–35 (see Robinson 1975; Bishop & Coulston 1993).

B: LEGIONARY CENTURION AWARDED WITH *TORQUES* AND *ARMILLAE* BY MARCUS AURELIUS

Traditional awards of *dona militaria* (military decorations) were still made by Marcus Aurelius and the chaotic Marcomannic and Sarmatian wars provided numerous recipients. This winter scene is inspired by Dio's account of the defeat of the Iazyges on the frozen river Danube in 172–73 (Dio, 71.7). Here Marcus Aurelius comes forward with hand outstretched to greet a surprised legionary centurion as a fellow-soldier (*commilito*). Aurelius' senior advisor, Claudius Pompeianus, carries the soldier's awards – *torques* and *armillae*. Both men wear the typical garb of the Roman general, muscle cuirass with fringed pteruges, and sash (*cinctorium*) to indicate their rank.

The centurion is identified by his long-sleeved red tunic. He is heavily bearded as was the fashion at this time. His helmet is a bronze Imperial Italic H, the last in the exceptional series of legionary helmets developed from Gallic

Relief of three legionaries from Croy Hill, Antonine Wall. Probably cut from a gravestone, it may represent a father (centre) and his sons. They are equipped with heavy *pila* and cylindrical *scuta* and helmets. All three wear the *paenula* cloak; the left figure has padded armour. Mid-2nd century. Now in the Museum of Scotland, Edinburgh. (Drawn by Steven D.P. Richardson)

Distance slab recording the construction of 4,140ft of the Antonine Wall by legio II Augusta, and showing the Capricorn and Pegasus emblems of the legion, c.142. (Hunterian Museum, University of Glasgow)

prototypes since the mid-1st century BC. It is uncertain if centurions still wore transverse helmet crests (Vegetius, *Epitome*, 2.14). He wears an old-fashioned ring-mail shirt with shoulder doublings, an armour popular in the 1st century AD but some shirts could still have been in service. His baldric and belt follow the example from the soldier's grave at Lyon, probably dating to 197. This style of belt and broad baldric, with strap-ends decorated with terminals, was popular throughout the 3rd century. The letters on the belt spell out FELIX VTERE – 'use with good luck'. His elaborate scabbard chape follows an example from Saalburg and his sword is the proto-pattern welded example from Canterbury. He also wears heavy leather gaiters which double as greaves. The trident and dolphin shield emblem follows a design on one of the Aurelian panels reused on the Arch of Constantine. It is uncertain if it was an actual shield blazon or simply the result of the sculptor's imagination. (See Wuilleumier 1950; Bennett 1983; Bishop & Coulston 1993.)

C: ROMAN PATTERN-WELDED SWORDS, 3RD CENTURY AD

It has been suggested that the sword became a secondary weapon in the 3rd century, legionaries relying on a thrusting spear until it shattered in combat and only using the sword as a reserve weapon (Stephenson 1999: 70–5). This is nonsense and the development of beautiful pattern-welded swords by Roman smiths in the late 2nd century AD indicates the continuing primacy of the *gladius* (this simply means sword, not short sword) as the legionary's close-quarter weapon. Pattern-welded blades were formed around a core of multiple iron bars with differing carbon contents to produce different tones, twisted into a screw then hammered and folded countless times, providing a strong yet flexible core to which hard cutting edges were welded (top & bottom right). The process meant that every sword was unique, while the mysteries of its production and the presence of orichalcum inlays of divine figures (here in the most basic form, left) suggest a closer relationship with the sword, perhaps even a degree of veneration.

The top three swords have also been forged with fullers, grooves running the length of the blade, imparting extra

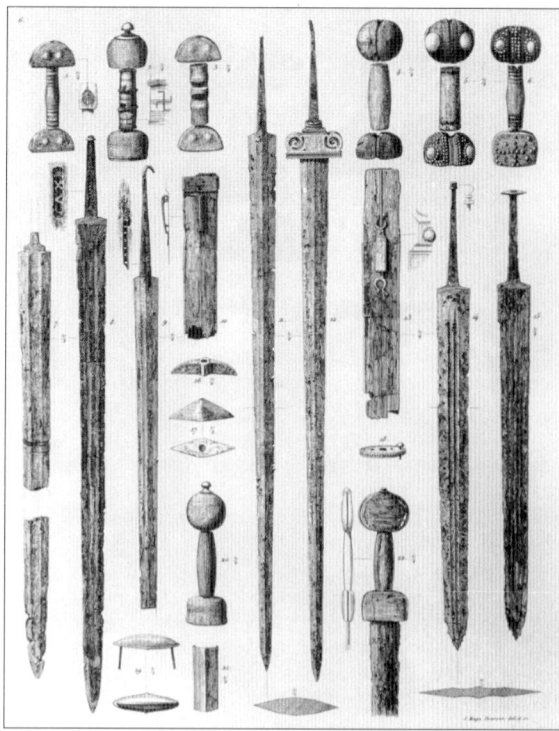

Roman swords of 3rd century date from Vimose, Denmark. From Engelhardt 1869.

strength, while the hilt detail illustrates the typical Roman form, here decorated with silver bands after an example from Illerup in Denmark.

Interestingly, more Roman swords have been discovered in Danish bogs than in the entire territory that the Roman Empire covered. These swords were probably not taken as booty from the Empire, but reached Barbaricum via highly illegal but widespread trade, and soldiers retiring to their homelands. These weapons found their way into the hands of warring factions and the huge numbers of swords from Illerup, Nydam and Vimose appear to have been taken from them when they were defeated and deposited in the bogs as offerings to the gods (Engelhardt 1865 & 1869; Ulbert 1974; Ilkjær 1989; Horbacz & Oledzki 1998).

D: ARCHERY PRACTICE

Vegetius informs us that legionary recruits were given some training in archery (*Epitome*, 1.15), and although archers are only attested in legio II Parthica, finds of archery equipment at various legionary sites suggests that *sagittarii* (archers) were not limited to II Parthica. Here we see Aurelius Maius, II Parthica's archery instructor (*CIL* VI 37262, AD 222–35), berating a *tiro* (recruit) who has scorched his hand whilst attempting to loose off a fire arrow. Maius' fine baldric with an embroidered dolphin follows the example from Nydam and he carries a *vitis* appropriate to his rank of *evocatus*, a veteran praetorian retained in service by the emperor on specialist duties and ranking only below a centurion (Dio, 55.24.8).

The incendiary-holding arrowheads are illustrated (right), along with trilobate and bodkin type heads, secured by socket or tang. The Roman bow was a powerful weapon with an

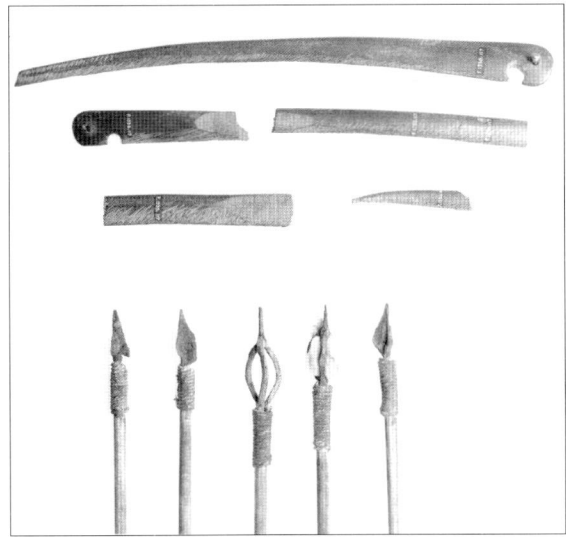

Barbed and incendiary-holding arrowheads and antler bow laths from Bar Hill fort, Antonine Wall, mid-2nd century. (Hunterian Museum, University of Glasgow)

effective range of up to 100m and maximum range of about 275m. The bow was built around a thin wooden stave with horn laminations on the belly (facing the archer) and sinew on the back (side facing the target). Drawing the bow compressed the horn belly and stretched the sinew back creating massive tension that was transferred to the arrow when the string was released. Reinforcements of bone or horn known as laths were positioned at the grip and ends of the bow to prevent it snapping under pressure. The bottom left detail illustrates the bone rings used to draw back the string, a method known as the Mongolian release. The broken ring at the far bottom was discovered at Dura-Europos, which fell to the Persians between 255 and 257. (See Coulston 1985; James 1987.)

E: MAXIMINUS AS *DUX RIPAE* WITH HIS BODYGUARDS, DURA-EUROPOS C. AD 232

The towering central figure is based on the portraiture of the emperor Maximinus (235–38), who may have been the first *dux ripae* ('commander of the river bank/frontier') at the key fortress of Dura-Europos in Syria during Severus Alexander's Persian War (231–33; note Herodian, 7.8.5). Maximinus entered the army as a common soldier in the late 2nd century, probably winning transfer from a cavalry unit to the emperor's horse guards (equites singulares Augusti), and progressing to the primipilate and then the equestrian military commands. After his possible command at Dura he was *praefectus tironibus* ('prefect over recruits') for the field army mustered to fight the Alamanni in 234. With these young soldiers supporting him Maximinus seized power in 235. As a professional soldier he was the first emperor to fight in battle and by so doing he set a dangerous precedent that no later emperor could ignore. Here he wears garments appropriate to his high equestrian rank, a tunic with purple stripes (*clavi*) usurping senatorial insignia, purple-fringed cloak and gold ring, the badge of soldiers promoted to the equestrian order (Herodian, 3.8.5). Maximinus still retains his old ring buckle belt and rather

Altar dedicated to Mars, Minerva, the Campestres (goddesses of the parade ground) and other gods, by Marcus Cocceius Firmus, centurion of legio II Augusta. The form of the altar and inscription suggests that Firmus served in the Imperial horse guards (*equites singulares Augusti*) before promotion to a centurionate in the legions. Mid-2nd century AD. (Hunterian Museum, University of Glasgow)

plain *spatha*, emphasising that he remains a *commilito* ('fellow-soldier') of the ordinary rankers.

The bodyguard to the left is a legionary from one of the Syrian legions. His finely painted *scutum* – modelled after an unfinished example buried under the Roman counter-wall at Dura during the Persian siege of c. 255/57 – has a lion motif perhaps connected to legio XVI Flavia, but the last legionary presence attested in the city is of IV Scythica in 254. This *scutum* was lighter than earlier examples weighing about 5 kg, and edged with rawhide instead of iron or bronze. His belt and baldric fittings follow finds from Dura. The spear (*hasta*) is based on a large triangular head from Saalburg; the painted shaft is suggested by depictions of decorated spears in the *Notitia Dignitatum*, an early 5th-century register of Roman officials and military commands. Contemporary

Antoninianus of Gallienus, showing the possible radiate lion emblem of the Praetorian Guard, AD 258–60. (Hunter Coin Cabinet, University of Glasgow)

Sestertius issued by Caracalla *c.*214–17, showing the emperor addressing his troops. The soldier on the far right carries a cylindrical *scutum*. (Hunter Coin Cabinet, University of Glasgow)

images of praetorian *pila* show a similar pattern but this might actually indicate binding to reinforce the shaft (Plate F). His tunic, with applied darts at the shoulders and bands and the hem and cuffs, follows a find from Dura but we cannot be sure that it was a military tunic. His loose trousers follow the type worn by soldiers on painted frescos from Dura.

The bodyguard to the right is based on the funerary relief of Aurelius Alexianus, a Spartan who served in a special cohort raised by Caracalla for his Parthian War (216–217; *ILS* 8878). Alexianus is shown wearing a *pilos*, the traditional felt cap of the Spartan hoplite and an apparent garment with horizontal bands, here interpreted as a cuirass of *lorica segmentata*. He also carries a heavy club – on the gravestone it is an attribute of the god Hercules but here becomes a *fustis*, the riot baton of the Roman Army. His baldric fittings also follow Dura finds, but the fine scabbard, made entirely of ivory except for a gold rivet at the centre of the typical disc-shaped chape, is based on the sword from Khisfine in Syria. As an elite soldier, and with increased pay as a bodyguard (*singularis*), it is not impossible that he might possess such an expensive scabbard. It might even have been a reward for bravery. (Bishop & Coulston 1993)

F: PRAETORIANS ATTEMPT TO CAPTURE THE EAGLE OF LEGIO II PARTHICA, IMMAE, AD 218

In 218 the emperor Macrinus was faced with a challenge in the form of Elagabalus, promoted as the illegitimate son of Caracalla by Julia Maesa, Caracalla's powerful aunt. Her wealth secured the defection of many legions, including II Parthica, still based at Apamea in Syria. Macrinus retained the support of the praetorians (he had been praetorian prefect prior to arranging the murder of Caracalla) and marched out to face Elagabalus' forces near Antioch in April.

The praetorians normally fought in heavy scale armour and with cylindrical *scuta*, but Dio reports that Macrinus had them fight without armour or the heavy *scuta* (perhaps of a more substantial construction than the Dura example). Dio tells us that the praetorians had the better of the fighting and forced Elagabalus' army into retreat, but for some reason Macrinus panicked, and fled from the battlefield so that Elagabalus was able to rally his army (Dio, 78.37). It is probable that the praetorians, disgusted by Macrinus' cowardice, defected to Elagabalus for they were honoured during his brief reign. Macrinus was captured by a centurion whilst attempting to cross the Hellespont into Europe and executed. Elagabalus, however, was insane and was murdered by the praetorians less than four years later at Maesa's bidding. An unpublished gravestone of a soldier of II Parthica indicates the precise location of the battle – the inscription says he was killed at Immae.

Here we see the praetorians (right), still equipped with their *scuta*. The shield emblems are derived from moon and star motifs well known from 1st-century depictions of praetorian shields and 3rd-century funerary monuments. In the 1st and 2nd centuries the praetorians' emblem was the scorpion, but here the shields carry the lion emblem shown on the coins issued by Gallienus to honour the praetorians for their role in his victories over Germans and usurpers in 258–60. Their heavy *pila* have bands of decoration shown on numerous praetorian funerary reliefs. Binding seems more likely than painted decoration because a few *pila* are shown with what appears to be cord wound around the shaft. This would partly be for grip but perhaps also to reinforce the shaft and prevent it splitting on impact. The praetorians wear regular ring-buckle belts with long strap-ends and wide baldrics with typical roundel and open-work decorative plates, but their medium-length swords have hilts in the form of an eagle's head and neck. These swords were the preserve of guardsmen and senior officers and were probably gifts from the emperor.

The praetorians are attempting to capture II Parthica's *aquila*, actually a live eagle in a cage! This is shown on the funerary relief of Felsonius Verus, *aquilifer* of II Parthica who died during Gordian III's Persian War (*AE* 1991: 1572). We do not know if the praetorians and II Parthica actually met in the battle, but they were the respective elites of their opposing armies, and considering the close ties between the units – many soldiers were closely related – it would not be surprising if there was a bitter fight between them. The *aquilifer*, conspicuous in his red tunic and bearskin (he ranked only slightly lower than a centurion), is defended by *lanciarii* (three soldiers at bottom left) who are armed with light *lanceae* javelins. One has been hit by a *pilum* and his javelin quiver is visible on his back. The quiver is suggested by the funerary portrait of Aurelius Mucianus, trainee-*lanciarius* in 215–18 (*AE* 1993: 1575). The other legionaries fight with heavy *pila* decorated with long streamers, following the example on the gravestone of Petronius Proculus, a tribune's clerk, who was with the legion at Apamea in 231–33 (*AE* 1991: 1686). All the legionaries carry oval shields edged with rawhide and medium-length swords. The gravestones from Apamea suggest that disc-shaped scabbard chapes were most popular, and all the soldiers wear the usual ring-buckle belts and carry heavy daggers. (See Balty 1988; Balty & Van Rengen 1993)

G: FRONT RANKERS OF LEGIO II TRAIANA ATTACK PERSIAN CATAPHRACTS, BATTLE OF RHESAINA, MESOPOTAMIA, AD 243

In 238–39 the Sassanid Persians overran the Roman province of Mesopotamia, encompassing parts of modern Turkey, Syria and Iraq. Civil war and Gothic attacks on the Danube meant that the Romans could not respond effectively until 242, and in 243 under the command of the praetorian prefect Timesitheus the Roman field army won a notable victory against the Persians outside Rhesaina. No details of the battle survive except for a passing comment in Ammianus mentioning it as a great Roman victory (Ammianus Marcellinus, 23.5.17), but we also possess possible evidence of the recruitment of new recruits to replace the casualties sustained by legio II Traiana in the battle (Fink, *RMR* 1971, no. 20).

Here the legionaries have feigned a retreat drawing the pursuing Persians on to hidden spikes and caltrops. These lame the horses and, as the Persian pursuit is thrown into utter chaos, the Romans turn and attack (cf. Herodian, 4.15). The Persian is based closely on a graffito of a cataphract from Dura-Europos, indicating a combination of mail and plate armour. His helmet is based on the example worn by a Persian soldier lost in the fighting in one of the siege tunnels at Dura in 256–57 (James 1986). The rider is secured by a saddle with four horns which grip him firmly, meaning he can fight effectively without stirrups. The scale horse armour is based on Roman examples from Dura.

The first rank of legionaries are equipped after a sculpture of a legionary from Alba Iulia in Dacia (Romania). The figure has a cylindrical *scutum*, a unique form of *lorica segmentata* with only three main girth hoops, and *manicae*, an articulated guard for the sword arm. Although broken, the sculpture

suggests that the figure wore a scale hood. Similar head protection is well known from the Dura frescos, but it is possible that the sculpture originally showed a helmet worn over the hood. The hastily painted legend on the shield reads: LEGIO II TRAIANA, BRAVE, GERMANICA (a battle honour granted during Caracalla's German war) AND GORDIANA (lit. '[emperor] Gordian's own'). The second-rank legionaries have scale cuirasses with finely embossed chest plates worn over an arming garment with *pteruges* for protection of the upper arms. Their helmets follow Robinson's Auxiliary Cavalry types but such helmets were clearly employed by both cavalry and infantry. Note how the throat flanges on the cheek pieces and the prominent cross-pieces on the bowl are designed to deflect blows. They defend themselves with the more common oval shield. (See Coulston 1995; Robinson 1975)

H: LEGIONARY, MID TO LATE 3RD CENTURY AD

The figure follows the funerary portrait of Aurelius Iustinus of legio II Italica (*CIL* III 5218). He was killed during a war against the Dacians and is shown grasping his sword hilt while his shield and *pilum* are slung over his back. The slightly dished shield decoration follows an example from Dura-Europos. The detail illustrates the plank construction of these shields, which had iron reinforcing bars and stitched-on rawhide edging. Iustinus' *pilum* had a single weight and was probably a socketed type as illustrated here. The details show one socketed and two tanged *pila* shanks from Saalburg in Germany, dating to *c.*260. The *pilum* shaft is bound with cord after the fashion depicted on some praetorian gravestones. His massive sword is based on an example from Nydam and, despite its length, the long triangular point suggests it was a cut-and-thrust weapon. The sword detail shows a contemporary long sword from Nydam, with a slim, tapering, almost rapier-like blade and rhomboid in section. Such weapons have been likened to the rapiers of the 16th century. His belt illustrates an alternative method of securing the ring buckle, which was to remain the mark of the soldier until the close of the 3rd century. The dagger detail illustrates and typical *pugio* from the Künzing hoard (Germany, mid-3rd century), a weapon which had been adopted from Spain in the 3rd century BC and remained remarkably similar to its ancient prototype. The short mail shirt has decorative borders of bronze rings, a feature noted from a shirt discovered at Vimose in Denmark, and worn over a padded arming garment, necessary to absorb the shock of blows and prevent the mail from being driven into the flesh. The detail illustrates a pinned hinge from Vimose, and indicates the manner in which Roman shirts would have been secured. Finally, the two helmets illustrate typical headgear between 260 and 300. The upper bronze helmet with its single bowl construction, and probably manufactured in a small military workshop, was abandoned unfinished at the fort at Buch in Germany *c.*260 in the face of Alamannic attack. The iron helmet follows the spangenhelme from Der el-Medinah in Egypt (*c.*300), a far simpler piece, composed of many small sections and riveted together. Such helmets were adopted from the Sassasians and became the norm for Roman troops; cheaper and easier to produce, they replaced the traditional single-bowl helmets and were churned out by state-run arms factories (*fabricae*) of the late Empire. (See Engelhardt 1865 & 1869; Ulbert 1974; James 1986; Bishop & Coulston 1993)

INDEX